The Lost Shanties
of Ribblehead

THE BOG CART

SATURDAY NIGHT AT BATTY GREEN

THE LOST SHANTIES
OF RIBBLEHEAD

W R MITCHELL

FOREWORD BY PETER CARDWELL
(Northern Archaeological Associates)

Many of the episodes in domestic life which
have come to light...since the beginning of
the Settle-Carlisle railway, might form
thrilling themes for the novelist.

Lancaster Guardian.

CASTLEBERG
1996

For
RUTH ANNISON
a tireless worker for the Settle-Carlisle

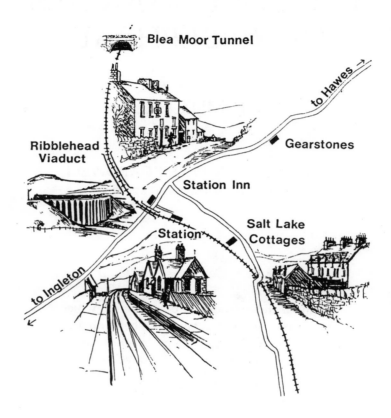

A **Castleberg** Book.

First published in the United Kingdom in 1996.

Copyright © W R Mitchell 1996.

The moral right of the author has been asserted.

ISBN 1 871064 83 X

Typeset in Palacio, printed and bound in the United Kingdom by Lamberts Printers, Station Road, Settle, North Yorkshire, BD24 9AA.

Published by Castleberg, 18 Yealand Avenue, Giggleswick, Settle, North Yorkshire, BD24 0AY.

Contents

Illustrations

Front cover: George Horner, former signalman at Blea Moor, completing a model of The Contractor's Hotel, the caravan which appeared at Ribblehead in the autumn of 1869. (Photo: W R Mitchell).

Back cover: Ribblehead Station, showing the 'down' platform. The station buildings, which have been dilapidated for years, are to be restored in 1996. (Photo: W R Mitchell).

Drawings of navvy life by Betty Harrington (courtesy of the Museum of North Craven Life). Other line drawings from Williams's *The Midland Railway: its Rise and Progress* (third edition, 1877). Picture map of Ribblehead drawn by Janet Acland.

Author's Notes

BATTY GREEN was the name most frequently used for the main settlement at Ribblehead, though it was referred to as Batty Wife Hole in the Census returns for 1871 and for early railway-related entries in the Burial Register of Chapel-le-Dale Church. A variation in the Burial Register was Batty Wife Green!

My account of life in the hutments has been built up from material collected over many years. Local newspapers, and especially contributions by "Rambler" to *The Lancaster Guardian,* were a prime source. Wildman's *Settle Almanack* for the 1870s had an annual update of Settle-Carlisle activity. A graphic, if semi-fictional account of incidents from the domestic life of navvies was published in *Chambers's Journal* (March 8, 1873).

As I began to prepare this work, it was stimulating to meet Northern Archaeological Associates as they compiled a Topographical and Archaeological Survey of the Batty Moss Settlements.

Foreword

THE SHANTIES AT RIBBLEHEAD were associated with the construction of the Settle to Carlisle railway between 1870-1875. This was the last major navvy-built railway in Britain, and two major engineering projects, the building of the viaduct at Ribblehead and the tunnel at Blea Moor to the north, required large numbers of navvies and their families to be temporarily settled at these remote locations. Nine separate shanties were erected in the vicinity and consisted mostly of rows of wooden huts. Their appearance was compared at the time to the gold diggers' villages in the colonies or the frontier towns of the Wild West. The shanties were dismantled upon the completion of the railway, and only occasional foundations of some of the buildings are visible today.

It is appropriate that it was on the "desolate moor" adjacent to Ribblehead Viaduct, while undertaking an archaeological survey of the surviving remains of the shanties on behalf of the Yorkshire Dales National Park, that I first met the author. I was immediately made aware of the depth of his knowledge of all aspects of the history of the Settle to Carlisle Railway, on which he has already written a number of books, and of the navvy settlements at Ribblehead in particular. It is accordingly gratifying to know that his knowledge of these shanties has now been drawn together in a single publication.

The contents of the book are based upon years of meticulous research, mostly from local newspapers produced at the time of the construction of the railway, but also from census returns, burial registers and records of inquests. This has enabled an informative account of the daily life at the settlements to be pieced together. The account includes descriptions of the work of the navvies on the viaduct and tunnel, as well as the quarries at Littledale, the brickworks at Sebastopol and the tramways that linked all of these locations—work which was both hard and dangerous, and involved a constant battle against the natural elements. The author's research has also enabled a detailed picture of the domestic life of the navvies and their families to be built up. The men and women recorded in the administrative documents of the railway company or census returns are brought to life as individuals, revealing their home lives, entertainment, romances and not infrequent lawlessness (more often than not as a result of drink), as well as their religious worship, sickness, and ultimately death—over two hundred graves at Chapel-le-Dale being a testament to the fact that the shanties could be both an inhospitable and dangerous place to work and reside.

Although the shanties at Ribblehead existed only some one hundred and twenty years ago, we have little detailed information regarding their layout and appearance. Indeed, there are no contemporary photographs of the navvies themselves and the shanties appear incidentally in only a single photograph of the viaduct under construction—which is ironic considering that the Ribblehead viaduct is probably now the most photographed viaduct on the British railway system. While the recent archaeological survey has provided the first detailed record of the surviving remains of the settlements, it is the research by the author that has enabled the life of these lost shanties to be so graphically brought back to life in this book.

Peter Cardwell
Northern Archaeological Associates.

Introduction

"Say—My Name's Sharland!"

THE west wind plays a tuba solo at the high arches of Ribblehead railway viaduct, in North Yorkshire.

A relief signalman who parks his car at the north end before following the trackside to Blea Moor box has to fight against the blast of air which sweeps up Lunesdale and Chapel-le-Dale, meeting its first real obstruction where the *Midland* line to Scotland is supported by piers of dark limestone.

Years ago, the children of families occupying the railway houses between the signal box and Blea Moor tunnel, walked to and from Ribblehead to catch a bus on schooldays. Before turning into the wind at the viaduct, they put stones in their raincoat pockets to stop them flapping.

Ribblehead viaduct, its feet resting on bedrock and its twenty-four arches clamped by mighty embankments, stands at the meeting place of the winds.

In the days of steam locomotion, men on gale duty at the north-end of the viaduct had to tighten up the tarpaulins of the wagons before a train crossed. Even so, tarps were pluck-ed away, to be blown like autumn leaves and to come to earth—a windfall in a literal sense—on the doorstep of a grateful farmer. A gale might put such pressure on a locomotive and rake of cattle trucks that the train was brought to a halt.

I was allowed to walk across Ribblehead viaduct when the line was closed for repairs. The westerly gale buffeted the parapets, which deflected it above my head. One of the daft stories of the Settle-Carlisle is of the ganger who, while cross-ing, had his cap blown from his head. The cap swirled through one of the arches and landed back on his head. His only complaint was that it was now the wrong way round,

9

with the neb at the back.

Originally, the viaduct was named after its location—Batty Moss. A "moss" in the Pennine context is swampy ground colonised by sphagnum moss, a great peat-forming plant. The Victorian railway-builders (1869-76) encountered banks of peat up to nine feet thick. The dry ridges were covered by peat and the crowing of cock grouse—*kowa, kowa*—was heard on every hand.

Contemporary accounts tell of railway workers plodding calf-deep through mire. The Contractor used a bog-cart, a light chassis fixed to a barrel, such as had been used agriculturally since the eighteenth century. It travelled smoothly over the wettest ground. The luckless horse ran the risk of breaking its limbs. Today, near Pier 13, is a memorial to railway workers old and new and an engraving shows the contrast between a Victorian navvy with a shovel and today's workman with a power drill.

The land west of the viaduct has been little disturbed and is pock-marked by swallow-holes. To the east, there are humps and hollows. The route of the main tramway is clear to see as it climbs from Batty Green to the scars. From here, a visitor has a panoramic view of Pennine ridges and that glorious trio of hills—Whernside, Ingleborough and Penyghent, each of them clearing the 2,000 ft contour.

Whernside is whale-backed. From its flank pours Force Gill Beck, which the railway-builders neatly diverted that they might take suitable dark limestone from the bed of the stream. Ingleborough, flat-topped and buttressed by lesser fells, and Penyghent, sprawling like a lion in repose, are but remnants of a land gouged and smoothed by water and ice. The local glaciers also daubed the terrain with a porridge-like mush we call boulder-clay. It was to test the resolution of the railway-builders, being hard as concrete in dry weather and sloppy after a spell of rain.

Walk along the tramway as the best introduction to Ribblehead. In spring, there will be a few larks in the sky. From the moor edge comes the reedy call of the lapwing. The Swaledale-type sheep stand and chew their cud while waiting for you to move on. The men who laid the tramway were said to have laboured like Yankees. A Contractor's locomotive was horse-drawn from Ingleton along Chapel-le-Dale, passing close to the little church where the yard would be extended to accommodate the dead of the railway shanties.

The tramway system not only conveyed blocks of limestone from Littledale to the base of the viaduct; it also transported coal from Batty Green to feed the vertical steam engines at the shaftheads of Blea Moor. On Saturday afternoons, the trucks were cleaned, in a fashion, and the train used as a Shoppers' Special, taking the womenfolk of the hutments to the shops and services of the Green.

A walk along the tramway leads you close to a ruined lime kiln. Between here and the viaduct stood Sebastopol brickworks, with two chimneys, ten kilns and rows of drying sheds for bricks made of local clay to line the arches of viaduct and tunnel. Notice a heap of discarded bricks, some fused together, others blackened and yet others cracked where pebbles formed areas of weakness. Local bricks were found to weather rapidly. They would be replaced, where they were exposed to the weather, by imported red or blue bricks.

From the tramway, stand and take in the impressive view. The viaduct is backed up by flat-topped Ingleborough. In "railway time", when few sheep were kept and the area was well-keepered, Ribblehead was empurpled in late summer by the flowering of the ling. The husky voices of grouse were heard on every hand.

Nothing remains of the Blea Moor hutments. Archaeologists plotted what remains—the foundations of huts at Sebastopol, a shanty near the viaduct, and marks on the ground near the junction of the old turnpike with the Ribblesdale road to indicate the varied activities at Batty Green.

Sebastopol and Inkerman are names associated with the

Crimea, where British and Russian troops faced each other and a hastily mustered team of engineers and navvies created a railway between the anchorage for the supply ships and the Front. The hutment of Jericho stood near the mouth of the tunnel. Jerusalem was on slightly higher ground, and on top of Blea Moor, where the brick shaftheads look from a distance like inflamed sores, were Tunnel Huts, their inhabitants dedicated to keeping the steam engines chugging as men and supplies were lowered down the shafts and debris from the workings brought up.

On a day when the sun played hide and seek in low cloud, I explored what remains of a self-acting incline connected with the two sections of a millstone grit quarry which was opened up by a Contractor desperate for sand to be used in the making of mortar and concrete. Laden trucks coming down the incline drew up the empty trucks. From that tramway there was a clear view to Denthead viaduct and the Settle-Carlisle running on a ledge cut from the flanks of the fells, notably the great hill called Knoutberry, named after an alpine plant, the cloudberry.

After many years of research, I can now ''put a name'' to many an old-time railman, going up the social ladder from navvy to John Crossley, the *Midland's* top man in the district. This notable engineer delayed his retirement so that he might oversee the construction of the Settle-Carlisle.

I think of John Ashwell, of Kentish Town, who was awarded Contract No 1 at the usual ''specification and tender'' terms but was persuaded by Crossley to reduce the figure somewhat. Ashwell soon found his outgoings were exceeding incomings. The weather was at its Pennine worst. The labour force was fickle. Building the railway dragged on much longer than planned and Ashwell faced bankruptcy.

The *Midland Railway*, well-aware of the reason for his plight, and acknowledging that he had done his best, took on the work themselves and ensured that Ashwell was not left pennyless. The *Midland* had little spare cash as they expanded during an inflationary period. The estimate for building the Settle-Carlisle was £2,200,000. The actual cost was £3,467,000, which worked out at £47,500 for each of the 72 miles.

The Settle-Carlisle roll call includes Edgar Ferguson, the engineer in charge from Settle to Denthead, and William Thompson, tunnels inspector at Blea Moor and Rise Hill. Among the "civilians" were Mr Tiplady, the Missionary appointed by the Midland in conjunction with Bradford City Mission. He was tipped over in love by a lady whom he married and bore off to milder climes. John Mather, of the *Welcome Home* inn, died miserably under the wheels of a cart at Ingleton as he made a desperate effort to stop a runaway horse.

In 1865, during the preparatory work, carried out amid a flutter of paper as the *Midland* took steps to secure the land granted to them by Parliament, Charles Stanley Sharland (surveyor) and his team plodded along the proposed route. He was mentioned once or twice, as Mr Sharland, by Frederick S Williams, in his history of the Midland Railway, published in 1877. Williams related how James Allport, the General Manager, and his Chief Engineer, John Sydney Crossley, first cast their eyes over the terrain, concluding that the one practicable route would use two north-south valleys, Ribble and Eden, linking them with a difficult and expensive traverse of high Pennine country between Ribblehead and the summit at Aisgill.

Allport, who was called—but not to his face—the Bismark of Railway Politics, had a flying start to his railway career as a protegy of George Hudson, the nearest the Railway World had to a king. John Crossley, a Leicestershire man, prepared the appropriate plans. The two men walked most of the seventy-two miles between Settle and Carlisle. Allport recalled: "We found it comparatively easy sailing till we got to that terrible place, Blea Moor. We spent an afternoon there looking at it. We went miles without seeing any inhabitant, and then Blea Moor seemed effectually to bar our passage northward.''

According to Williams, "the first pioneer sent into this remarkable country" was Mr Sharland. A Tasmanian by birth, he had been for some time professionally engaged on the *Maryport and Carlisle Railway*. "Immediately on his appointment, he started off to find the best route for the proposed line, and in ten days walked the whole distance from Carlisle to Settle, taking flying surveys and levels...''

Sharland and his men were snowed up at Gearstones, near Ribblehead, for three weeks. The landlord, Francis Yates and his family, fed the Midland men on eggs and bacon, varied by—bacon and eggs. When supplies dwindled, Sharland made a tunnel through the snow and the marooned party drank from a horse-trough.

Williams recorded that Mr Sharland and his staff, while surveying in an oakwood on the Newbiggin estate in the Eden Valley, were approached by the landowner, William Crackenthorpe, who asked "in a somewhat decided tone" what they were doing on his property. They mentioned the proposed new railway line from Settle to Carlisle and that their present plan was to go through the wood. Mr Crackenthorpe was "as indignant and excited as a benign old gentleman with a frilled shirt front could be expected to be", and Sharland did his best to pacify him.

Later, Allport and Crossley, being in the neighbourhood, called on Mr Crackenthorpe, "the Druid-like reverer of his ancient oaks," to placate him still further. Their courtesy seemed to impress him. A meeting between the four men was arranged at the disputed oakwood. Mr Crackenthorpe had one condition to make—that the *Midland* men would spare the largest and finest tree in the wood. This was readily agreed. Why was he interested in that particular tree? Said Crackenthorpe: "So I might hang you and all the engineers of the *Midland Railway* upon it, for daring to come here at all!''

No other railway writer had mentioned Sharland. In 1975, while researching the history of the railway, several of us who formed a centenary committee under the Settle Civic Society were thinking of writing him off as a myth when the telephone rang at my home in Giggleswick. An Antipodean voice said: "Say—my name's Sharland." It was Michael Sharland, nephew of the railway engineer, ringing up from Tasmania, having heard of our plans to celebrate the Settle-Carlisle's hundredth birthday.

Charles Stanley Sharland was not, after all, a figment of a railway historian's imagination. Through the post, in due course, came a photograph of Sharland as a young man. He looked astonishingly young to be given such responsibility by one of the premier railway companies. The photograph had been taken in London in October, 1869. It was the time when the civil engineering at Ribblehead began with the arrival of the first engineers and their men. They set up a base in a four-wheeled caravan beside the old turnpike.

Sharland was not to experience the heady days of railway construction. Gravely ill with tuberculosis, he withdrew from the Settle-Carlisle, moved to Torquay and died there on March 31, 1871, aged twenty-six. Despite his brief encounters with the Settle-Carlisle, he has become a prominent part of its folklore.

It was also in 1975 that I met O S Nock (known to his friends and associates as Ossie), who was kept abreast of our committee's deliberations. My home overlooks the Settle-Carlisle just north of Settle. Ossie, on a visit, knelt down facing east, across North Ribblesdale to the big railway embankment leading up to Langcliffe. Ossie was not paying homage to the Settle-Carlisle but attempting to relate its gradient to our window ledge (which he presumed was horizontal), trying to detect the 1 in 100 which Young Sharland and his fellows decreed should be the ruling gradient for there to be a smooth crossing of the watershed at Aisgill.

Ossie's grasp of railway matters and his lucidity in talking about them were evident when he attended two of our pre-centenary meetings, at Carlisle and Ingleton, on the second occasion deputising for Eric Treacy, the Railway Bishop, who was indisposed.

Treacy was available to give the major speech at the centenary lunch in a marquee erected behind the main station building at Settle. The Bishop spoke about railway matters with an evangelical fervour. Was it not he who had listed, as the greatest wonders of the north-country, Hadrian's Wall, York Minster and the Settle-Carlisle, and not necessarily in that order?

The story of how the Settle-Carlisle line came into being, a consequence of inter-company rivalry, has been oft-repeated. Briefly, the *Midland* could reach Ingleton on its own metals and there had to hand over passengers and traffic to the *London and North-Western Railway,* a rival for the Scottish traffic. By negotiation, the *Midland* tried to get access to Carlisle but failed in their attempts and in 1866 they obtained parliamentary powers for the construction of the Settle-Carlisle. The first sod was cut in November, 1869. The works were let in four main contracts, No 1 taking in two immense engineering projects—Ribblehead viaduct and Blea Moor Tunnel.

The Lost Shanties of Ribblehead is mainly about day-to-day life in the hutments which during railway-time (1869-1876) were strung like wooden beads along a strip of land from Batty Wife Hole to Blea Moor. The main settlement, Batty Green, was near the road junction.

Work began as a matter of urgency where major feats of engineering were required. At Ribblehead, on the ridge of land dividing the watershed of the Ribble from that of Littledale Beck, a viaduct with flanking embankments would carry the line across the dalehead at an elevation of just over 100 feet and Blea Moor would have a hole blasted through it with the help of a new-fangled explosive called dynamite.

James Ashwell, the Contractor, had to concentrate men at Ribblehead, an area where there was just a sprinkling of farms, and an urgent necessity was to provide living quarters for the men and their families.

Into being came the hutments which are frequently referred to as "shanty towns" and have been compared, in their appearance and the life they supported, with the new settlements of the American West. Living at Batty Green, Sebastopol, Inkerman, Jericho, Jerusalem and Tunnel Huts were colourful characters, including Welsh Nobby, Leeds Polly, Nebby Scandalous and Devon Sam. It was estimated in the 1870s that about 2,000 people—railway folk and locals—resided between Horton-in-Ribblesdale and Denthead.

A contributor to *Chambers's Journal* (1873) set the scene magnificently: "It came in the way of my work recently to visit a colony of navvies engaged in the construction of the heavest portion of the works on the new line of railway at present being made between Settle and Carlisle. The headquarters of this scattered colony are on the slope of an outlying buttress of Ingleborough Hill, at the foot of which is a deep hole in the limestone, whence issues the headwaters of the Ribble. From some old legend of a suicide, this wild and savage place bears the curious name of Batty-wife-hole.

"Three or four hundred navvies are housed in the wooden huts, covered with black felting, that have been set down at hap-hazard on to the slope above the river-head, and there are various settlements bearing outlandish names bestowed upon them by the navvies themselves. Inkermann, Sebastopol, Belgravia, Jericho, Salt Lake City—all these can be reached with no greater exertion than half an hour's wade through the deep, treacherous, oozy bog of which much of the moorland is composed. True, when reached, they are not much to look at, but they are racy of phases of that curious half-savage navvy life, which has in it so much that is interesting to the student of the by-tracks of human life."

In due course, the hutments were dismantled and taken elsewhere. Cleansing winds swept away all but faint traces of where they had stood. The subject of these moorland communities continued to enthral me. They have also fascinated writers, artists and musicians. I was emotionally roused by a stage play, *Head of Steel,* which is Julia Darling's dramatic reconstruction of shanty town life, when Sophie Weston, who is in charge of music at Catteral Hall, the preparatory school of Giggleswick, arrived at my home with an offer I just could not refuse.

This was to narrate *Running on Rails,* a cantata specially written for the school, on its sixtieth birthday, by Jan Holdstock of Leeds. It would evoke "navvy time". The world premiere of *Running on Rails,* at the Northern Preparatory Schools' Music Day, was given by a choir of 120, with Simon Lindley, organist and choirmaster at Leeds Parish Church, as the conductor. With piano and drums providing an accompaniment, and Simon urging the young choristers to ever-greater efforts, the songs lived.

"Seventy Two Miles of Rail" ended with an appropriate *shhhh* (as the locomotive came to a halt at Carlisle). "Pennine Weather Song" contrasted languid summer days and a winter during which the snow "freezes and it flurries". I recalled to myself winter days, with a fringe of icicles on the water tank at Blea Moor, a brazier burning beside the water crane and locomotives fitted with snowploughs lumbering towards Dent Cutting.

As narrator, my greatest moment came in the run-up to a calypso referring to "a wonderful new invention, costing £200 per ton" which "was transported by road to the hills for blasting the rock...its name was Dynamite!" A second later, Simon and the children began "Dynamite Calypso" with an appropriate explosion of sound.

It was fascinating, during the £3m restoration of Ribblehead viaduct, a few years ago, to visit a modern "shanty". The Victorian workmen had occupied long wooden huts, and

were plagued by sparrows and rats. The modern accommodation consisted of several metal porta-buildings, which
arrived in sections on the backs of special lorries. Some were
allocated to the civil engineers, under Tony Freschini, and
became offices. Only one was permanently occupied, most of
the workers using the mobility of cars and vans to commute
to distant places like Leeds and Northwich.

A team of scaffolders remained on the site. Their "hut"
needed an extra bed and they made one from—scaffolding.
This bed had a tubular metal frame and a plank. The scaffolders provided themselves with a shower, fed by water
from a plastic tank on a tower improvised from scaffolding.
They decorated the walls of their temporary home with col-
our pictures of young ladies in saucy poses, the pictures rip-
ped from magazines and calendars. The men had rigged up
an aerial to watch television.

When the restoration was completed, the "shanty" was
moved by lorry with little fuss. Those who dismantled the huts
in the 1870s made a thorough job of it. When the Yorkshire
Dales National Park commissioned a topographic and archaeological survey of *Batty Moss Navvy Settlements,* in 1995,
it was carried out by Northern Archaeological Associates.
Robert White, the National Park archaeologist, and a team
under Peter Cardwell, studied, measured and recorded the
visible traces. Little remained after 120 years of blustery winds
and the freeze-thaw effect of the High Pennine winter.

This recent activity at Ribblehead—and the recollection of a
long-distance telephone message, "Say—My name's
Sharland"—has stimulated me to gather together into book
form the facts and figures about Ribblehead's transient
population of railway-builders and their families. I was specially interested in how a "semi-wild" labour force was brought
under control by Contractor, Parson and Magistrate. The
shanties were not lawless for long, simply because Victorian
morality, and stern punishments meeted out in the Police
Courts, quickly brought any wrongdoers to heel.

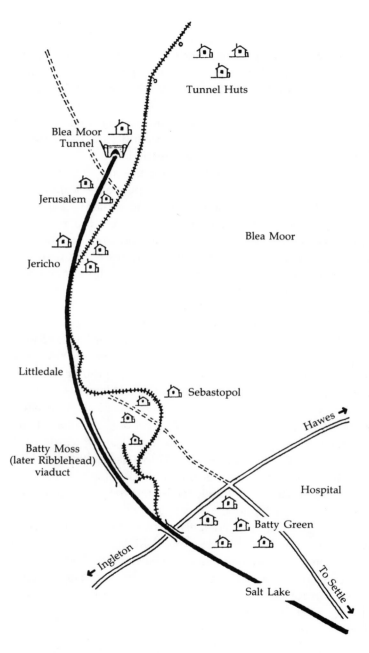

Ribblehead—supposed sites of shanty towns

The Desolate Moor

The country through which the line passes is amongst
the wildest and most romantic in England...the change
from the moorland and fells of the southern part to the
highly-cultivated and Devonshire-like Eden Valley is
extremely striking.

Westmorland Gazette, May, 1876.

INGLETON, a village with Ingleborough Hill as a
backdrop, was already familiar with the toot of a steam
locomotive when work began on the Settle-Carlisle line.
The Clapham-Lowgill line crossed the valley of the Greta on
an immense viaduct which was the demarcation between two
forceful railway companies, the *Midland* and the *London and
North Western.*

Rivalry between them had led to the proposal for a Settle-
Carlisle line and, the *Midland* being able to operate as far as
Ingleton on its own metals, it was convenient for men and
supplies for the new railway to be off-loaded here and routed
along part of the Lancaster-Richmond turnpike, which was
now something over a century old. In the summer of 1870,
the Ingletonians were deprived of sleep, the streets being
alive, night and day, by carts heading for the railway hutment of Batty Green.

The intrusion had begun in December, 1869, when a trac-
tion engine, dispensing showers of sparks and smoke, and
towing a four-wheeled caravan, climbed Storrs Brow from
Ingleton. A tale spread through the district that they had
come all the way from London. The van was to accommodate
engineers and their helpers, one of whom dubbed it The Contractor's Hotel.

Ten men ate and slept in the van through the winter. One man shudderingly recalled: "A tight fit it were, surely. Of a night I used to have to stand by for half an hour with a bull's-eye (lantern) as a guide to the men homecoming through the waste. Sometimes a man would stick. His mates would have to dig him out. There were two chain o' knee-deep water four times a day for the fellows atween their meat and their work."

Their task was to make preliminary borings for shafts which would go deep through the peat to bedrock so that the big viaduct might take shape without delay. A farmer who heard about the proposal to build a railway in these parts said: "They'll hev ta build it on stilts." Donkeys were used as pack animals to transport tents, food and equipment to Blea Moor, where shafts were needed to increase the number of working surfaces when the tunnel was being excavated.

Where is Ribblehead, the source of the famous river? As marked on the map, it is situated at a spring which bubbles up from between limestone rocks between Batty Green and Gearstones. An old-time description is that "the water issues from two openings in the limestone rock with a grassy mound in the centre, and then after purling over a bed of pebbles for about twenty yards it drops with a jingling sound through various openings and continues its course for some distance underground."

Ribblehead was in Contract No 1 (Settle Junction to Dent Head) for which fourteen firms tendered. The Contract was awarded to the much-respected John Ashwell, of Kentish Town, North London. His figure of £349,226 was considered by John Crossley to be somewhat excessive. As already noted, Ashwell revised it downwards to £336,523. The *Midland* engineers appointed to Contract No 1 were R E Wilson and E O Ferguson.

The railmen who were first to arrive at Ribblehead saw dozens of swallowholes and an elliptical pothole, Batty Wife Hole, containing a pool. In local folklore, these holes were the vents through which water poured to soak the world at the time of the Biblical flood. They remained in case the Good Lord wished to give humanity another lesson in humility. A curious tale connected with Batty Wife Hole is that of Mr Batty, a bootmaker, and his long-suffering wife. As Mrs Batty returned home in a blizzard, she blundered into the hole, which became a watery grave.

Another tale relates that Mrs Batty, having been regularly thrashed by her husband, left home. He implored her to return. They arranged to meet at the Hole for a chat, hoping their differences would be reconciled. Mrs Batty, finding herself alone, drowned herself. Mr Batty, arriving a little later and sensing what had happened, flung himself in the pool.

Ribblehead, where several valleys meet, was a playground of glacial ice which, on melting, left the "basket of eggs" effect of a big drumlin field. A Pleistocene chill is experienced hereabouts for most of the year. No one who knows Ribblehead would be surprised to see snowflakes in summer. The wind is funnelled up Chapel-le-dale with a banshee wail. John Ruskin, storm-battered, looked up at Ingleborough and wondered how the mountain could stand without rocking. Blea Moor sprawls across the valley head. Big and rounded, it resembles an upturned pudding dish.

In winter, this was a desolate scene. In summer, there were moments to uplift the heart. A Wesleyan local preacher, setting off on a preaching jaunt to the hutments on an August morning later confided to his diary that the sunshine had revealed the full beauty of "nature's picture gallery". He rejoiced at the memory. "Hill and dale, heath and meadows, all looked charming..." He saw, in one sweeping view, Ingleborough, Whernside, Penyghent, Fountain Fell, Pendle Hill, with other hills too numerous to mention and, being a devoted Christian, added: "Who with a soul to appreciate so beautiful a creation, could refrain from saying: 'What a privilege to be a man'."

Midland men who set to work at Ribblehead itself found

themselves ankle-deep in heather and under the suspicious gaze of Mr Farrer's gamekeeper. For years, only the whistle of the farmer to his sheepdog or the crackle of gunshot on the Glorious Twelfth, the opening of the grouse-shooting season, had disturbed this area. Way back, there had been an annual sale of vulgar (black) cattle driven down from Scotland and assembled on on the moor within easy distance of the beer-barrels and whisky bottles of *Gearstones Inn*. At Sleights, roadmen looking for material with which to patch up the turnpike, found evidence of life much further back. A heap of stones was found to hold a stone coffin containing a skeleton. The roadmen broke up the coffin to use the stone on the road. The bones were given to Richard Clapham of Austwick Hall, a local antiquarian, who presumably studied them.

Surveyors, spearhead of the Midland assault force, completed their work. Suddenly, Chapel-le-Dale was alive with traffic. The road declined into "pools of water, loads of mire, deep and long cart ruts." A parochial report from Ingleton criticised the contractors and hoped that an early agreement would be reached about mending the roads.

"A Grumbler at Bad Roads" in a peevish letter to the *Lancaster Guardian,* mentioned its miry condition, adding that "the mud waved and dashed against the splash-boards of a carriage as if it had been travelling in the bed of a river of mud." This was a byroad, maintained privately, which led to the little farms snuggling against Whernside. It was the handiest way to reach the southern end of the proposed Blea Moor Tunnel.

The farmers had allowed the road to be used on the promise that it would be repaired when it had served that purpose. "This promise has not been fulfilled, and our district surveyor of the Settle Highways Board should at once look after this matter, as they are the custodians of our public highways. The farmers in the neighbourhood are quiet men and such lovers of peace that although they grieved at the worse-than-ploughed-up roads which lead to their farm-steads, they still let their disapproval end in words..."

At the start of 1871, the old turnpike had degenerated into a strip of ground with holes and ridges, ruts and hollows, pools of water and rolling mud. To avoid using the road, the walker had to climb tottering walls, skip over turbulent becks and walk over rugged pastures. It was dangerous for carriers, difficult for carting and virtually impassable to pedestrians.

A man who had known the road for fifty years said there were no words in the English language to describe its bad state of repair.

THE CONTRACTORS' HOTEL

During "railway time" there was a grouping of buildings near the junction between the Ribblehead road and the old Lancaster-Richmond turnpike, also beside the tramway, at a point where a branch line would lead to the base of the viaduct. An artist is not bound by historical accuracy and this lively drawing gives a hint of the bustle at Ribblehead as the big viaduct (seen distantly) took shape. The Contractor's Hotel is shown on the right.

Navvies at Home

There is enough felt on the huts of Contract No 1 to make a path from Settle to Carlisle, six feet wide. This requires tarring three times a year.

Lancaster Guardian, 1873.

THE NAVVY was the most lowly of many categories of workmen employed in building a railway. Other manual workers were masons and miners. A worker out-of-doors dressed to keep warm. A miner in Blea Moor tunnel needed tight-fitting clothes to prevent drag.

No photographs of Settle-Carlisle workmen have been found but, judging by the appearance of contemporary lead-miners and quarrymen, who worked in the locality of the Settle-Carlisle, the typical worker wore coarse shirt, a cravat of coarse-weave material to absorb the sweat, a jacket, sometimes a waistcoat and fustian breeches, held close to the legs by yorks (leather straps) extending round the leg just below the knee. Boots and clogs were among the most numerous items of footwear.

Itinerant workers usually kept their possessions to a minimum, but the most self-respecting of men would at least have a change of clothes for off-duty wear or when attending a Sunday service at the Mission or a grand concert, such as that which took place in the Schoolroom in November, 1874, when "the room was crowded to excess, though the prices of admission were, front seats 2s.6d and the second seats 1s."

An urgent requirement was for lodgings to attract and hold the workforce in a remote area where farms, inns and cottages were thinly-spread. The men must be within walking distance of their work. A namesake of the author, William

Mitchell, a labourer who travelled from the Isle of Dogs, in London, was lucky to find lodgings for himself, his wife and four children, with John Morphet, of Lower Scales, Ingleton Fells. The family re-union began with tragedy. When Mrs Mitchell arrived at Ingleton by a *London and North Western* train, she found one of her twin children (who had been weak from birth) was dead. She mentioned it to no one until she reached her destination, at Mr Morphet's farm, where she discovered her husband had left to lodge at one of the cabins near Batty Wife Hole. An inquest was held. Mrs Benson, who had "laid out" the child, said there was no bruises on it. The Coroner's verdict was "died from natural causes and not from violence".

An early arrival, Mary Blake, had tramped from London to Ingleton. Here she became drunk, kicked up a row and was apprehended by PS Wildman, making a considerable noise as she was taken to the lock-up (referred to in a contemporary account as "gratuitous lodgings"). On the following day, Mary appeared before the Rev R Denny and fellow magistrates, who fined her five shillings and costs. In default, she would have to go to prison.

The answer to an acute shortage of accommodation was for the Contractor to provide wooden huts, the value of which had been proven on many another civil engineering project. By July, 1870, over forty huts had been erected. The number grew steadily and before the year ended accommodated 700 men. The number under cover by the time of the 1871 census was over 900. The siting of the huts depended on the state of the ground and the main work areas. They were also adjacent to the main tramway running from Batty Green to the summit of Blea Moor.

So whereas Batty Green was a main service area, Sebastopol was handy to the viaduct and Jericho, at the southern end of Blea Moor, would accommodate the men working in the Littledale quarries (from whence came limestone for the viaduct) and in the tunnel, where there was a preponderance of miners. An early account refers to the settlement just south of Blea Moor as Winterscale Huts, after the name of a local farm. Though it is not known for certain, Jerusalem and Tunnel Huts would be placed where vertical steam engines took over from locomotives to haul up the laden wagons. A large hutment appeared at Dent Head, its workers concerning themselves with the north end of the tunnel and a viaduct.

Most of the huts simply rested on the ground, with nothing special in the way of foundations. As they were sited outside the area purchased by the *Midland* from James Farrer of Ingleborough Estate, for the course of the line itself, Farrer was able to augment the initial income of £1,702 by charging hut rents. The poorest workers would make their own lodgings, with low stone walls, timbers raised like the ribs of a wigwam and a coverlet of sods. It is known that at least one family who had been allocated a hut took in lodgers, had a "tommy shop" (provision place) and accommodated any of their children who were married in vans which stood beside the parental hut.

Any navvy who, through drunkenness, was not permitted to enter the hut where he lodged might cat-nap in the nearest engine shed, where it was warm and dry. On several occasions, a home-going toper, overcome by drink and weariness, lay down on the driest place he could find, which happened to be the tramway, sometimes with fatal results as he was run over by a locomotive.

Two types of huts were erected—a large type with three sections, one being the sleeping quarters of the family who had been allocated the hut, the central area a combined kitchen and dining room and the far section for the lodgers who were accommodated with little thought of space and hygene. A visitor to this type of hut mentioned six lodgers were being accommodated. The lady of the house did not intend to be spoken of as being measly with food, for "her notions of my capacities for rashers of bacon eaten along with buttered toast must have been based on her experience of navvies." The commonest type of the first 100 huts to be erected at Batty Green held eight men. Felt was stretched across the roof and boiling tar applied to the felt to provide additional rainproofing.

A newspaper man of 1871 wrote that though the "hut villages" of Batty Green, Sebastopol and Jericho were upon a dreary moor far away from the busy marts of commercial men, still there is no lack of roast beef, savoury pastry, luscious fruits and beveridges of pleasant flavour to lovers of the bottle. Tradesmen and pedlars swarmed about the hutments like bees round a hive. A Methodist preacher who visited the area in 1872 was surprised that drapers, tea dealers, shoe merchants, clock and watch dressers went "from house to house and from railway village to village" with their merchandise on the Sabbath Day as on other days. The author of the annual update on Settle-Carlisle progress in *Wildman's Almanack* (1873) described Batty Green or Batty Wife Hole as "a town of felt huts, with surgery, tommy shop, hospital, reading room and schools, the last three being provided by the company." The iniquitous "truck" system applied. A Contractor paid his men in token money which could only be exchanged for goods at their own tommy shops.

The workers of Batty Green did not keep fashionable hours and rarely arrived back at their lodgings warm and dry. A visitor to Batty Green during the winter of 1872-3 who watched navvies returning from work noted that "the face of the swamp in the watery twilight was alive with navvies... They stalked carelessly through the most horrid clinging mire. What thews and sinews, what stately, stalwart forms, what breadth of shoulder and shapely development of musicle were displayed by these homecoming sons of toil."

It was the wife or lodging-house keeper who held together this random collection of railway workers. One middle-aged housewife was referred to as "a robust, powerful, purposeful dame, of immense energy, considerable surface roughness and real genuine kindliness of heart." The women appear to have had the verve and determination shown by women in the American West, which was still being "tamed" at the time the Settle-Carlisle was under construction. A visitor to Ribblehead in 1872 referred to the wives of railway workers as being "hardy". They were also hut-proud, adorning the wooden walls of the huts with paper hangings and pictures cut from illustrated newspapers and periodicals. "They make substantial meals, keep good fires and study the comfort of their lodgers." Most of the navvies, being decent folk, washed and tidied themselves before sitting down to a good savoury meal. The men then read newspapers (made available free of charge by the Contractor) or formed themselves into musical groups, some choral, some instrumental.

The 1871 census is our first detailed record of those who lived at the shanties of an area then known as Ingleton Fells. The entry for James Tiplady, "home missionary", is of special interest. Tiplady, and two others who witnessed to the power of religion on the Settle-Carlisle, had been appointed by the Midland in consultation with the Bradford City Mission. Tiplady was responsible for the spiritual welfare of those engaged on Contract No 1 and a Mr Hancock, based at Kirkby Stephen, dealt with Contract No 2, which began north of Denthead.

Tiplady, who was 23-years-old at the time of the census, would have had a positive, Bible-based, slightly melodramatic view of religion which would be well-suited to workmen and their families, who would like plain speech. Tiplady was quartered at No 3 Batty Wife Hole. There was a lodger, 21-year-old Jane Herbert from Essex, and a servant lass, 16-year-old Eliza E Combs. In the realm of religion, John Ashwell the Contractor helped where he could. A Methodist local preacher was busy soul-serving in summer, when a visit to the heights of Blea Moor was tolerable. Quakers, with well-developed consciences, attempted to teach the navvies how to knit.

The Methodist preacher jotted down impressions of the shanties. "While passing the numerous huts, one could not but notice the pigs, ducks and hens wandering at large on the moor, showing that the railway operatives, however unfavourably circumstanced, cannot rest without they are surrounded with the domestic animals."

The tramway, beside which most of the workforce lived, had been a vital early requirement, the first stretches being laid at the rate of a mile a week. Steam-hauled trucks moved people, equipment, supplies and coal. It collected dressed stone from Littledale for the emerging viaduct and, from Ribblehead, transported locally-baked bricks to line the tunnel workings. That tramway made clever use of the contours, though in places the gradients were as steep as 1 in 16. Between Sebastopol and Jericho, the tramway crossed a ravine on a wooden frame. Eventually the tracks stretched for two and a-half miles from Batty Moss to Blea Moor and, with the branch lines and sidings, had a total length of four miles. What is taken to be Belgravia, a posh suburb of Batty Green, appears as an incidental feature on a photograph of the partly-constructed viaduct (about 1873). Here were rows of huts and and a few individual dwellings with porches.

Mention has already been made of the traders and dealers who arrived at the shanties, usually from Ingleton, following the rutted road up Chapel-le-Dale. Every Saturday afternoon, a train started from the Tunnel at 2pm to take people to buy a week's provisions at Batty Green. Known as The Market Train, it had an engine and two wagons. The passengers were asked to sit in the bottom of the wagons.

The construction of the railway was an opportunity for Messrs Burgoin and Cocks (a name which varies in its spelling in contemporary accounts, the alternative being Burgoyne) to become large-scale grocers and provision dealers. Mr Burgoin was the practical man and Mr Cocks dealt with financial aspects. The partners developed their enterprise so rapidly that in 1871, within a year of it being started, they moved into splendid new premises in Duke Street, Settle—and marked the occasion by giving away 500 glass cream jugs and sugar basins.

At Settle, using two large ovens, Messrs Burgoin and Cocks produced 4,000 loaves of bread daily. They had a large "butching shop" where each week the stock slaughtered consisted of four fat cows and from ten to fifteen sheep, besides "porklings and fat pigs". From a commodious warehouse at Batty Green, the firm also distributed newspapers and periodicals. The warehouse was used for a "large party and dance" when, in the summer of 1873, a party from Settle, having been given a tour of the works, gave an evening concert which was followed by high jinks. Burgoin and Cocks did not have a monopoly for among the retailers at Batty Green was an innkeeper and grocer named John Clark Garlic.

Living conditions in the huts were cramped. In 1874, the Medical Officer of Health for Sedbergh, visiting Denthead, found that some of the huts had been set on marshy ground where (as he reported) there was "no vestige of drainage save the open trenches cut around the walls of the huts to protect them from inundation." The huts were approached on planks or stepping stones. The Medical Officer estimated that the cubic space for each occupant in the sleeping apartments were very much below 300 feet, "the minium required for the maintenance of health." In one hut, five bedsteads were jammed so tightly together that the sleepers in the furthest beds had to clamber over the others. And, reported the shocked official, no provision appeared to have been made for the separation of the sexes.

A visitor to Batty Green during the winter of 1872-3 afterwards wrote for *Chambers's Journal* a somewhat romanticised account of his meeting with a navvy family whom he called the Pollens. The account captures the spirit of time and place. The old couple had a "tommy shop". A married daughter lived at the gable of the parental hut, which was divided, with communicating doors, in the usual way, one room being occupied by lodgers. The visitor described what he called a "navvy ball".

There was a tap at the door communicating with the room inhabited by the lodgers. "Sundry smothered and gasping squeakings of a fiddle had been audible from that apartment...Mrs Pollen shouted "Come in". Enter a stalwart navvy, blushing from ear to ear, yet there was a twinkle in the big black eye of the good-looking fellow." He bore a message from the navvy brotherhood in the other room that they might share in the festivities of the evening. They would contribute music and refreshments. And they would be on good behaviour.

The navvies trooped in, sat on the extreme edge of a form and accepted with gratitude Mrs Pollen's offer of wine. The black-eyed navvy produced a pail of strong ale and a bottle of whisky. He played a lively tune on his fiddle, imperceptibly edging up to two of the lasses. He had loved Miss Pollen for a long time; they had "squared it together" and if her father had owned another van they might now be married. Then a smart ruddy-faced young man with black curling hair and the physical development of a Hercules sang *My Pretty Jane*. A dance followed with the black-eyed navvy managing to play and dance simultaneously. His big boots clumped noisily on the boarding of the floor. The beer pail was replenished. Everyone relaxed.

A thump on the outer door heralded the arrival of a grim-looking navvy in his working togs. He called himself the Wellingborough Pincer. A newcomer to Batty Wife Hole, he was very much the worse for drink. A Northamptonshire man, he had heard that Mr Pollen was from the same area, so he had come to pay his respects. He was welcomed and made himself at home. He also quaffed more than enough of the free ale to render him drunk and objectionable. The other navvies held their peace, out of respect to the Pollens.

Mrs Pollen settled the matter. Being on duty at the "tommy shop", and having been called away to serve some customers, she returned and quickly summed up the situation. Grabbing Pincer by the scruff of the neck, she threw him out of the hut. Harmony was restored—for a time. Pincer reappeared, seemingly in a penitent mood, though his eyes kept straying to the ale-can. He was allowed to stay.

Pincer, in his worsening condition, suddenly hit the ruddy-faced young man in the eye, also cutting his cheek-bone. He did not retaliate because he did not intend to brawl in the presence of women. The matter would wait until the morning. Mrs Pollen, grappling with Pincer, dragged him across the floor and ejected him. She shot the bolt on the door. Pincer could not return. He hammered on the doors and window shutters. He shouted abuse. Now it was Pollen's turn to retaliate. He called for Joe, a powerfully-built, red-eyed bulldog, and loosed the animal into the night. There was a dull thud and a gurgling noise. Pollen shouted: "Come, Joe" and the bulldog returned, wagging its tale. The door was shut.

Several days later, Mr Pollen received two summons, at the instance of Pincer, one for selling drink without a licence and the other for setting a dog on him. Then the Pincer called and said he would stay legal proceedings if the Pollen's dog was shot. The doctor had assured him that were this not done, Pincer's arm must inevitably be amputated. Mr Pollen would not hear of a compromise.

Pincer, in court, stated his case and summoned a witness who saw him being worried by the dog. Mr Pollen pleaded his cause. He cited his way to prove that she sold no drink but that the whole affairs was a "treat". Pollen, replying to a question by a magistrate, said he had called the dog in defence of his property. The Bench gave judgement against the Pincer on both counts.

The writer who heard the Pollen side of this sorry tale concluded his account by the relating that the Pollen conveyance, on its homeward way with passengers who included Pincer's witness, was upset in the ditch. The reason appeared to be "the collective inebriety of the passengers". At home, a triumphal entry was accorded to the Pollens. The "Wellingborough Pincer" returned to work a wiser if not a better man, but he was execrated by the whole community for having imported legal proceedings into a colony where the policemen lived in a sort of contemptuous toleration. Hints were uttered that his career at Batty-wife-hole would be a short one. The Wellingborough Pincer was last seen in the neighbourhood of a deep blind shaft that had been excavated to divert the water from the workings in the tunnel. "He may have suddenly migrated, but there are not wanting those who darkly hint that an exploration of the shaft would disclose the fact of his being in the immediate vicinity of its bottom."

This account, which today would be classified as "faction", was almost certainly based on a case which came before the Ingleton Bench in June, 1872, relating to Robert Holland, a provision dealer at Batty Green, who was charged on the information of the police with selling drink without a licence. Superintendent Exton conducted the case for the prosecution and the defendant had no advocate. The case depended solely on the evidence of Thomas Cryer, who said that on May 21, John White, Samuel Paradise and himself went into the house of the defendant at about 8pm. The house was full, as there were between twenty and thirty people. He saw glasses on the table. Some of the people were dancing and some were singing. He called for a pint of beer, which was brought by the defendant's wife, and she received threepence for it. He drank the beer and afterwards got several more glasses with the men who went in with him. He saw no other person pay for any drink, and the threepence he paid Mrs Holland was all he paid for drink.

Elizabeth Parsons, who gave evidence for the defendant, said that she went into Mrs Holland's house at about 10pm, when she noticed the complainant in the company. He was kicking up a row and Mrs Holland turned him out of the house. He then went to the back door and got into the house. Mrs Holland evicted him a second time. Cross-examined, she said there were about seven men and about as many young women in the house. She saw some glasses on the table with wine in, but she did not see the men have wine or call for any beer. Neither did she see anyone pay for drink. She herself had a little wine.

William Stafford, a lodger with the defendant, saw the complainant enter the house, though he was not in the same room. He did not see him pay for beer and he had not seen him drink any beer. He corroborated the last witness's evidence about the complainant making a disturbance and being turned out three times on that account by Mrs Holland. There were about fifteen or sixteen people in the house. The young men and women were enjoying themselves. Mrs Flower's daughter, who was an acquaintance of the Misses Holland, had come down from London and Mrs Holland was treating them. The drink was free.

The Bench suspended its decision on this case until it heard another case which arose from it, Thomas Cryer complaining that Mrs Holland put him out of her house, when he re-entered by the back door and was turned out again. Robert Holland, arriving home at about 10.30pm, said: "I'll shift you". He opened the door and set his bulldog on him. The dog tried to seize him by the throat, when he kept it off by his hand, which it bit in two places. Cryer showed his hand to the Bench, but some of the marks had disappeared. The defendant told the Bench he did not want a row and the complainant was kicking his house door. He said that Cryer had been fighting on the moor, but Cryer denied having fought that day. In the event, both cases were dismissed.

Snooping on railway huts was an unsavoury part of the policeman's task. Evidence of drink being supplied without a licence could be obtained by an official who was a stranger in the district. He would order drink and then charge the individual who supplied it. Usually, the local bobby and a colleague watched through the window of a hut at night.

In the summer of 1872, when the Methodist local preacher and a railway missionary were in the district, having a Sabbath-day walk over Blea Moor during which they had conducted outdoor services, they found the streets were "good and orderly". They had been rowdy on a previous visit. On this latest visit, in the evening the visitors saw a drunken man running about the hutment, being pelted with mud by big boys, "a sight which a number of spectators found hilarious." The poor man's face was covered with dirt. The amusement ended when a stranger checked the boys. Shortly afterwards, two men were apprehended for house robbery and carried away by the police to the Ingleton lock-up."

On May 20, 1872, a man had fever and headache, followed by an unsightly rash. His condition was diagnosed as smallpox. This viral disease broke out in the shanties of Sebastopol and Jericho. In a single week, the vicar officiated at five funerals in Chape-le-Dale church. It was claimed that most of the fatal cases in adults were from intemperance, and the Ingleton magistrates were criticised for granting so many licenses to vendors of beers and spirits on the hillside encampments. The authorities tried to stamp out illicit sales in the huts and, if any barrels of ale were found, smashed them up on the tramway.

In fact, living conditions at the hutments were restricted and insanitary. A commentator noted that "many of the huts are much plagued with rats, which have left the mountain stream on the moor close by to share the better things of human life." Any infected huts were limewashed. The drainage and ventilation were improved. Mr Ashwell arranged for sufferers to be moved to hospital—two detached huts, connected by a 20 ft long covered way, with space for ten patients. One hut was occupied by Mr and Mrs Halifax, who were trained nurses. A large oven was provided for baking the patients' clothes and convalescents had a small library.

Within a fortnight of its opening on June 8, the hospital was full. Of 35 cases admitted in the first month, nineteen were cured and discharged. Only three died. Edwin S Green, Medical Officer of the Temporary Smallpox and Fever Hospital at Batty Green, applied to the Guardians to enlarge it, to which they agreed. So another building, with a length of 48 ft, was added and ten more patients and an additional male nurse were accommodated. A washhouse and dead-house were added.

The navvy's hut was his castle—or her castle, in the case of Ellen Emmerton. She was assaulted by William Overman, who entered her hut, grabbed her and tossed her out into the road, knocking her on the back of her head with his fist and ruffling her hair. The Ingleton magistrates heard that Ellen clambered back into her hut and fastened the door. Overman opened a window and called her "bad names". For his defence, Overman said that Emmerton had behaved so badly to his mother she deserved to be taken to the police. She was drunk at the time of the alleged assault. Overman was fined 2s and ordered to pay 12s costs.

Anti-Irish feelings led to Thomas Brown threatening, on three occasions, to burn down an Irishman's hut. At Ingleton Court, with Mr James Farrer and the Rev R Denny on the bench, Elizabeth Murphy, wife of the complainant, said that she and her husband had taken the hut at Batty Green. On July 15, as they were thinking of going to bed, Brown and many more navvies arrived at the door and used offensive words. She asked what they meant. The men went away but returned. Brown and his mates called out: "Come out of that or we will fetch you out. If you are not out by four o' clock tomorrow, we will bring your things out and burn the bloody hut down."

Brown had an alibi, but could produce no witnesses as he was apprehended by PC Goodison. Mrs Murphy told the

Bench that her husband was Irish, but she was not, and she expected to be protected by the laws of her country. Superintendent Exton said that if he was to keep the peace, he must ask that such cases be severely dealt with. James Farrer said that Irishmen were under the same laws as Englishmen, and they had an equal right with them to be employed in this country. Brown was bound over to keep the peace for six months in two sureties of £50 each and himself in £100.

Actual assaults were quite common, with Winifred Reaves, a navvy's wife, being fined 20s at Court for assaulting another woman. Theft was a regular charge at Ingleton Court and was dealt with severely. Robert Gildey stole a coat and Henry Perry a watch. A driver employed by Mr Ashwell, the Contractor, returned home in 1871 to find among the missing items his wages, those of an eleven-year-old lodger, the driver's woman, a lodger and various objects from the hut. No one in the huts had seen the man and woman. So the driver and the lad set off to run to Ingleton, in case the missing couple were absconding, and hoping to arrive there in time to see who was catching the 10-10pm train for Leeds.

They were not far from home when they encountered a well-laden trap on its way to Wray. There was room for the boy; the man ran beside it, keeping up with the trap despite having to negotiate mud, ruts, ridges and unbroken stones. He ran in vain, for at Ingleton there was no trace of his women. The trail now led via Selside, Horton, Austwick, Bentham and Wennington, but all trace was lost. The driver telegraphed to the police at Barrow, to no avail. At Batty Green, sympathy for the driver evaporated when it was learnt that he had been living for three years with a woman who was already married.

The weather-gods of the Pennines threw at the navvies wind, rain, sleet and snow. On the night of April 17, 1871, they also contrived to deliver ''a sharp and decided shock of earthquake''. A strange rumbling noise preceded the shock, which was severe at Batty Green and even more so at Jericho, situated at the south end of the tunnel, where hut-dwellers awoke with a start as the earth shook. A woman compared the accompanying noise with the rumbling of a train through a tunnel in a town. Another, not finding a satisfactory explanation, sent her lodgers out-of-doors with lanterns to discover "the shaker of their hut". None was found. "At last they found that the door latch was deranged; but failed to detect the invisible agent that had tampered with it."

A lodger who had arrived at Jericho that night was standing outside the hut when the earthquake struck and he was thrown against it. His landlady told him a locomotive at the nearby engine shed must have burst. In a hut where pots and boxes shook with a noise "sufficient to awake and alarm the inhabitants", a woman awoke to find her bed shaking so violently she grabbed the bedposts. "Similar effects were produced on other persons. The indescribable noise which attended the vibration caused general alarm.'

At the end of 1871, the list of facilities at the shanties was impressive. A representative of *The Lancaster Guardian*, visiting Batty Green, was impressed by "the crowing of cocks, the cackling of hens, the noise of merry, fine-looking children...The tradesmen from various localities may be seen going from hut to hut, vending their multifarious merchandise, some of whom ply their trade on the Sunday. Potters' carts, brewers' drays, butchers' carts, bread carts, meal and flour carts, drapers' and grocers' carts, &c., are at intervals passing from Batty Green to Jericho and other hut villages." Batty Green sported a brewery, public houses, grocers, shoemakers, saddlers and other shops in abundance. "It would be a difficult matter for anyone to calculate the amount of meat and drink consumed in one week."

Early in 1871, the weather was grim and the labour situation desperate. Facilities were improved in the hope that more men would be recruited. A wooden building erected at the southern end of the tunnel became a Reading Room and

School, being inaugurated in style with a tea-party and entertainment.

The navvies were a sporty group. Almost from the moment when the first huts were erected at Ribblehead, the spare time of the liveliest group of men was divided between drinking and various sports. In March, 1872, there was a running match for the championship and £10. The spirit of the occasion was summed up by a correspondent of the local newspaper: "The road to Gearstones from an early hour of the morning showed by the number of vehicles and people that something more than usual was about to take place. At ten a.m., the crowds were immense. In fact, all business was at a standstill. Taking up our position at Gearstones and looking towards Batty Green, a wagonette and pair is seen rapidly approaching. This contained the cause of the excitement. Alfred Kellam and Samuel Barker were its occupants, and this immense mass of people had congregated to see them run.

"At eleven o'clock, both men were stripped and had taken up their positions, Kellam's fine proportions and elasticity of sinew being remarkably prominent, but Barker was not a whit behind; the betting was even. The pistol being fired, both got away in capital style, Kellam slightly leading from the first. At about 100 yards there was no perceptible difference. The betting then went rapidly up on Kellam, 3 to 1 could find no takers. The next and last 100 yards showed all the result of the finest 200 yards' race that this side of the county has ever seen. Kellam won by fully 3½ yards, and the race was run in 22 seconds. A collection was immediately raised for Barker, and three cheers given for both with hearty goodwill. Mr Hirst (the umpire), John Perkins (Kellam's referee), and James Moore (Barker's referee) received quite an ovation. The day finished up with various other sports, Kellam being very prominent in winning three other races."

The Lancaster Guardian noted in 1874: "It matters not what important things are going on, if there be sports within a few miles of the line, locomotives, tunnels, bridges, brickworks, &c will be deserted for the navvies' paradise. Wrestling, running, leaping, &c., must all be seasoned with a plentiful supply of drink. A dog fight or a man fight, which is sure to attend a drunken spree, is a favourite amusement. Men often fight with a desperation almost incredible, and woe to the man who dares to quell the affray. If report is not false, policemen often consider it prudent to keep out of harm's way. Round after round is fought, while backers and lookers-on clap hands, cheer, and curse and shout until the battle ground becomes hell for fierceness and passion. When the combatants have beaten and bruised one another until they are almost too weak to stand, the seconders will take them on their kees until their faces are sponged with water and drink is given to revive them. After a brief respite, the battle is resumed and the combatants, if they are what are termed men of pluck, will beat one another until they become too weak to stand, when the content for victory will be adjourned for another heat. To the credit of the navvies, good feeling returns when the fighting is ended.''

Lads played ''topple-stone'', each in turn hurling a stone at the topmost one in a heap, selected the tramway at the point where it crossed the road because it was firm and level. One of the lads was struck by an engine which arrived unexpectedly. His right leg was taken off at the hip. He astonished his relatives and friends by living.

Batty Green could muster enough men to sustain a cricket team. In August, 1874, a match was played against a team of workmen from the Settle end of the project. It was a low-scoring game, dominated by the bowlers. The key figures were Batty Green's Goddard and Dr Dobbie (8 wickets and 9 wickets respectively). Plank and Harrington bowled well for Settle. There were no fewer than ten ''ducks'' recorded in the game and the state of the wicket must be questioned. Reid and Plank were congratulated on reaching double figures. Needing 49 to win, Batty Green were 19 for 2 at the end. Had they gone on, a close finish would have been certain.

By 1875, shanty life was in conspicuous decline as work on the line was completed. Local people who had complained of the mess now feared an increase in the rates they paid for the huts which were being dismantled had a combined rateable value of £600. In the following year, Batty Green and its suburbs (to quote a local reporter) were much reduced in size. "Nearly all the huts are down and what are left will very shortly be demolished." J R Thomson reported on the last phase of shanty life: "On our way through the navvy town, whose wooden walls and felt-tarred roofs we had often noticed from the line, we had a chat with a blacksmith who told us that a fair number of railway employees are still left at Batty Green. The houses, he said, were comfortable, and the situation healthy, but it was lonely and 'hard to leave'. There was no place of worship now, and no school for the children nearer than Chapel-le-Dale."

THE CONTRACTORS' AMBULANCE

Danger—Men at Work

The greatest difficulty met with is the bad supply of
labour. Navvies and masons cannot be tempted to stop
on account of the damp climate.

Wildman's Almanack, 1873.

TIGER, Gipsy, Dagger, Belter, Punch—these were some
of the nicknames for men recruited to do the menial
work at Ribblehead. The most clannish section,
composed of "Liverpool-Irishmen", had worked on the
Mersey Docks. But English workers were more numerous.
They were among the 2,300 men recruited for the work on
Contract No 1, including Ribblehead. Englishmen and
Irishmen worked amicably together in the excavation of Blea
Moor Tunnel, differences being forgotten in the face of com-
mon danger in the dark, dank world of shafts and headings.

Navvy was a generic name for a workforce which had a
range of skills and included masons, brickmakers,
carpenters, miners, horse-keepers, mortar-grinders, cement-
burners and engine-tenters. They worked round the clock on
weekdays but never on Sunday, except at the special request
of John Crossley, the Resident Engineer. A visitor watched
some of the operatives digging, "some pulling down, others
building up, some sawing, some wheeling, some carting,
while the noise of hammers and other implements was inces-
sant."

Wages were paid on Saturday night. The total payroll for
around 900 workers between Batty Green and Dent Head, for
August 13, 1870, was in the region of £1,800, exclusive of any
sub-money (payment in advance) and the large sums claimed
by tradesmen, farmers and others who had carted materials

to the works. In 1874, Ingleton magistrates had to take quick steps when cases of forgery were reported to them, the defendants being miners in Blea Moor Tunnel who had tampered with their sub-tickets. Such a ticket was issued as an advance on wages, which by this time were being paid fortnightly. It was claimed that the men had altered the figures written on the tickets, to their advantage. The aptly-named John Money and Michael Nolan were each committed to the Assizes at Leeds, where they protested their innocence and the jury believed them. The judge concurred. Money was discharged and the case against Nolan was dropped.

The prosecution is of general interest because of the insight given into the method of payment. It was revealed by James Bennett, timekeeper at Blea Moor Tunnel, that Money had been working on his shift for about six weeks. On pay-day, which was Saturday, the men were paid up to Wednesday night. The subsequent three days were carried on to the next fortnight's account. Money, having applied for a sub-ticket for ten shillings, received it at the tunnel from Joseph Thomas Jones, assistant agent to the Midland Company, and was alleged to have changed the ten shillings to forty shillings.

John Ashwell, an experienced Contractor, transformed Batty Moss in a few weeks. He laid out a spacious workyard at one end of the Moss and set up service units—a blacksmith's shop, saw mill, carpenter's shed, stables, pay office and stores. Over 100 strongly-built horses were put to work. By 1872, the number of animals had risen to 130. Mr Ashwell ensured that they were "in prime condition". They showed by their glossy skins and well-rounded bodies that they were well-cleaned and fed. Horse-power, harnessed to the celebrated "bog cart" or to tip-wagons was soon to be seen in Littledale, a shallow valley on the flanks of Whernside and adjacent to the area where the largest civil engineering works—the viaduct and tunnel—were to be carried out. The Contractor had searched hard and long for a suitable quarry. Several trial holes had been sunk and the best source was found to lie beneath the bed of Littledale beck, which was promptly diverted to expose the stone.

At Batty Moss, it was deduced that solid rock lay some twenty-five feet down through peat and clay. A story began to circulate that the piers were being supported by bales of wool. In reality, Job Hirst and his son Walter, who would be directly responsible for its construction, set the foundation stones of the piers on a thick concrete base above bedrock, knowing that the viaduct would take at least 30,000 cubic yards of dressed stone. The first stone of what was originally known as Batty Moss viaduct, and would become the celebrated Ribblehead viaduct, was laid by William Ashwell on October 12. Mr Davidson, the Midland's inspector from Ingleton Road to Dent Head Viaduct, was a regular visitor.

The viaduct took shape, from north to south, with the scaffolding, heavy baulks of timber, being placed around groups of seven piers at a time. Each group was so swaddled until the arches had been turned, when the timbering was dismantled and erected for the next group. And so on. As the years went by, the northernmost piers had a light gantry, bearing rails for steam travellers (mobile cranes) while further south the piers were at various heights.

The toot of a locomotive was heard as yet another load of dressed stone was transported along the tramway and on to a siding leading up to the base of the viaduct. The dark limestone, the best stone available locally, was occasionally flawed and so eventually the area was littered with discarded blocks. From the twin chimneys of a brickworks, black smoke poured to be whisked away by the Pennine wind or, on calm days, to give the site a dark canopy.

An inquest held in 1874 into the death of Archibald Matthenson, a twenty-seven year old railway labourer who was judged to have died through an accident, provided an insight into the method of abstracting stone. On a Sunday morning, about 9am, Matthenson volunteered to take charge of a horse in the absence of a young man, and to draw some wagons laden with stone for Batty Moss viaduct to the point of the decline. He had moved one of the immense wagons, with from five to six tons of stone, and had detached the horse from it for its descent, when Peter McBride, the ganger, noticed him lying on the metals about two feet in advance of the descending wagon. He thought that he must either have fallen or been knocked down as he uncoupled the horse. McBride shouted to the fallen man to get out of the way, without response. Both sides of the tramway were so filled with stones that McBride could render no help. "The two perilous wheels of the wagon passed over the young man's thorax and crushed his head and lungs. He died immediately."

In 1872, the masons working on the structures of Contract 1 went on strike for more pay. They were being paid 6s.3d for a nine hour shift, with the addition of 8d per extra hour when they were called upon to work ten hours a day in summer. The strike lasted a week. Presumably, they had their demands for more cash met.

Anyone who ventured near Blea Moor heard the chugging of vertical steam engines, standing beside the tramway from Ribblehead which had been laid by those men who had "worked like Yankees". The engines needed a copious supply of water and coal, the last-named being originally transported in sacks on the backs of donkeys, then in wagons hauled up the steepest gradient by "crabs", and succeeded by wire rope and steam engine, as already applied on the north side of Blea Moor. Many of the wagons, though laden with coal, were crowned by bags of flour and other domestic commodities.

One who travelled on the footplate of a locomotive outward bound from Batty Green was to recall "the mist creeping along the hills, steam and smoke driven into one's face at times by the fell-country wind, the shrill whistling or screaming of the locomotive, the blazing open air fires at intervals along the route and the devils sending forth their lurid flames

at the various shafts up the ascent of Blea Moor..." The
locomotive lingered for water on the edge of a deep cutting
"and then passed over frail wooden bridges which spanned
some deep road or the chasm forming for the tunnel
viaduct."

A visitor to Blea Moor in the summer of 1871, when about
160 miners were at work sinking shafts and driving the tunnel, would be impressed by the continuity of the work, conducted by relays of men who relieved one another at 6am and
6pm. At first, gunpowder (also known as gun-cotton) was being used, filling holes made by hand-drilling and then ignited
by means of a time fuse. In that summer, Shaft A (at the proposed entrance to the south end of the tunnel) had attained
a depth of thirty-five yards. About a hundred yards had been
tunnelled northwards and lined with brickwork, the bricks
being produced in quantity on Batty Moss and positioned in
places to a depth of over two feet thick. Standing by the shaft
was a 12-inch winding engine which also worked an 8-inch
pump and an appliance which supplied the underground
workers with air.

No 1 shaft, which was permanent, to help ventilate the tunnel, was (by 1871) sunk to foundation level and miners had
excavated some forty yards each way, completing as they
went the brick lining. There was a continual racket from the
12-inch winding engine which delivered air to the workings
and removed any water which had collected. No 2 shaft,
which would also remain when the line was completed, was
down to foundation level, at 127 yards, and lined
throughout. Work was about to begin on driving the
headings through limestone and grit at an average speed of
about four yards a week. This being deeper than the other
shafts mentioned, a 16-inch winding engine was employed to
"draw up the debris". A 20-inch engine was in position for
working the 10-inch pump. "The water met with varies from
80 to 100 gallons per minute. It is a curious fact that if the
tunnel had been required to be of a few feet lower level, so

large a body of water would be met with that the greater amount of pumping power would be required than is at present employed. Engine power is laid down to raise 450 to 500 gallons per minute."

At the top of the Tunnel was a self-acting incline. As laden trucks came down, empty trucks were drawn up to a millstone grit quarry which had been opened up to obtain stone for concrete and sand. A Y-shaped quarry, with a few huts, scarred the moortop but without it sand would have had to be imported and the mortar, needed for work in the tunnel and for a large viaduct on either side of Blea Moor would be expensive. At the tunnel's north end, the air was supplied to the men working at the heading by "a simple and effectual contrivance, viz, a long column of water in a wrought-iron pipe, which has its outlet through a rose fixed on the pipe. The column of water has a pressure of 120 lb per square inch. Consequently, the rush of water drives the air up a pipe 11 inch by 9 inch to the face of the headings. The force of air is so strong that it will blow a candle out two or three yards from the end of the pipe."

If anyone visiting the works inquired how the Contractor had got such a bulky object as a locomotive to Ribblehead, it was explained that horse-power was used for the journey by road from Ingleton, with over thirty animals yolked to it for the ascent of Storrs Brow to Chapel-le-Dale. When the first locomotive was due to be moved, scores of Ingleton folk rose from their beds at 3am on a June morning in 1871, about which time (according to the *Lancaster Guardian*) came the tramp of Mr Ashwell's sleek-skinned and well-fed horses. "It was well for both men and beast that the weather was so fine, or the imperfect state of the road would have rendered the transit of the engine a difficult matter."

This incident proved to be Mr Ashwell's last cause for jubilation. In September, 1871, he was in serious financial trouble, defeated by the weather, the grim terrain and monetary inflation. John Ashwell had won the respect of the

Midland, who did all they could to help him, and of the men, who revered him. Ashwell always had their welfare in mind. He had provided them with the very huts they occupied and had arranged that "boxes" would be placed on the gantry at Ribblehead viaduct to give the men some bad-weather shelter. On the ground were sheds for the comfort of the masons.

Ashwell had paid his masons from 1s to 1s.6d a day higher than the wages of Lancashire or Yorkshire so that the daily pay of many of the masons was 6s.6d. It was not enough to hold the labour force, and every pay day one or two men indicated they wished to leave. They were replaced from a reservoir of spare masons. As many as eight fresh hands might be set on the works in a day. "According to the opinion of the foreman, it will be two years at the present rate of progress before the viaduct will be finished."

It had been John Ashwell who provided the Mission House. He had the typical Victorian class-consciousness, however, and when he had presided over a Penny Reading he comented: "There is honour due to the Batty Wife Greeners inasmuch as they are able to furnish such talent from the lower and working classes."

The *Midland* took over his contract, appointing as their agent a man with a similar surname—William H Ashwell. Work continued without a hitch. Charles and Walter Hirst were still busy working on the viaduct, which would absorb 3,000 yards of concrete as well as the vast quantity of stone, described in an account of 1871 as "black marble" which was "dug out of a quarry on Mr Farrer's estate". The tramway which transported building stone from the quarries impressed a newspaper correspondent, who wrote exuberantly: "How would moorland rustics of past generations stare and wonder if they could awake from their long resting beds and see an iron pathway up the steep mountain glittering in the sunlight and hear the clang of hammers, the tramp of horses, the crack of carters" whips, the noise of workmen, the braying of donkeys, grinding of machinery and the smoke of many fires?''

The "black marble" was not easy to work, being especially hard. The quarries were apt to be flooded and it was proposed to introduce a steam pump. In 1871, a visitor watched as blocks of limestone weighing up to four tons each were lifted by steam cranes operating on a gantry to where the masons awaited them. The cry was for stone, and yet more stone. The Contractor planned to use additional mechanised force so that double the number of workmen might be employed. About sixty masons were employed by the viaduct dressing the stone, "which requires much effort", the class of work being 18-lock in course. A 10hp engine worked continually mixing mortar, the lime used being Barrow Lime, from the neighbourhood of Leicester. Stone was raised to the required level by steam crane, two hand-cranes and their "travellers", by which the stone was turned and set.

Work went on along the whole route and by the autumn of 1871, about 150,000 cubic yards of material had been removed from the area south of Blea Moor to form cuttings. The number of men employed was about 150, though it fluctuated a good deal. The Contractor would have been happy to have doubled the number. Two locomotives were set to work hauling tip-wagons. The displaced material was dumped to form an embankment which would eventually extend to the northern side of the viaduct. Most of the work on this part of the line was let to gangs from Batty Green. The men divided their earnings equally among themselves in proportion to the hours they worked. "The men, on account of this co-operation, earn good wages and they might do well but for drink, which meets them at every step. They appear to be powerless to resist the British workman's greatest foe."

The horses used for the tip-wagons cost up to forty guineas, a considerable loss when (as happened with some regularity) animals met with an accident and had to be put down. A valuable "tip horse" lost its shoe and was replaced

LAYING THE TRAMWAY

temporarily by a "road horse", which had difficulty in moving the half dozen loaded wagons. "The horse managed without any mishap to tip four of them. The fifth wagon ran over one of its legs and cut it off, on which account the horse had to be killed." Another day, a horse which "got its legs entangled in a rope, which caused it to fall, was run over by a wagon. The injury was such, the horse had to be destroyed.

In March, 1871, Judge Ingham, sitting at the County Court, dealt with an action by Thomas Wood, a sub-contractor on the railway, who sought to recover from the defendant, an overlooker or manager employed by Mr Ashwell, the Contractor, the sum of £25 for damages, the defendant, having deprived him of the use and possession of a horse and for its detention. It was a complex case, but gave an insight into business practices of the time. Wood, having taken out a contract under Mr Ashwell, hired a horse from Thomas Pearson.

The defendant, who was named Moody, was asked by Wood to buy him a horse, which he agreed to do. An animal, bought from Richard Buckle for £12 was used by Wood until he was dismissed from his contract. For the defence, it was contended that the horse in question belonged to the defendant and was let on hire to the plaintiff at the rate of sixpence a day, the defendant supplying the corn. A fresh arrangement was subsequently made. Now the plaintiff was asked to pay 1s a day, and find his own corn. (The verdict was for the defendant, with costs).

The tramway soon claimed a victim, Annie Wall, a girl who had travelled from London with her aunt, Mrs Powell. They lodged the night at Sebastopol, and caught a tramway train just before noon on the following day. The locomotive was drawing three laden muck wagons and Annie sat in the first of them. When the locomotive was derailed, she was thrown from her seat, along with material from the wagon, being scalded and suffocated.

In September, 1871, George McConnell, an eighty-six year old itinerant razor grinder, wanting a lift by tramway, and disregarding a caution that he must sit in the bottom of a wagon, perched at one end. After a quarter of a mile, the point being set wrongly, the driver of the train pulled up and reversed. On re-starting, McConnell was jerked and fell, being caught between two buffers. He was unconscious when picked up and taken to the *Welcome Home* at Batty Green. He subsequently died. In 1892, an inquest held at Batty Green concerned a man who left the *Railway Inn* the worse for drink, fell asleep on the tramway and was decapitated by a train returning from Jericho.''

To ride in a locomotive between the viaduct and the tunnel was a thrill for people attracted to the works by their scale and variety. In 1871, this befell a man who reported on the sensation for the *Lancaster Guardian*: ''When leaving the viaduct, my guide hailed an engine driver who was about to return with a train of empty wagons to one of the cuttings in the direction of the tunnel. After mounting the engine and taking our position, so as to support ourselves by the brass rail on its side, the snorting steed started off at a tolerably quick speed. No one can imagine the queer sensation which comes over one from the rolling and pitching potion of the locomotive caused by the unevenness and crookedness of the tramway, excepting a novice in such a mode of transit. Up and down, heaving on one side and anon on the other, slackening its speed at curves, and then accelerating it when they were past, was enough to make nervous persons giddy and to relax their hold.''

Near the tunnel was a large wooden viaduct, with openings between the sleepers ''wide enough for a corpulent boniface to drop through.'' Early in 1872, a locomotive and three wagons were crossing the viaduct when the last wagon ran off the metals and plunged into the void. All the wagons were derailed. ''Had not the coupling chain snapped, the locomotive and the men on it would all have been whirled into the tremendous opening.'' The main losers were Messrs Burgoin and Cocks. ''In the wagons were half of a fat cow, a fat sheep and other merchandise to the value of £16. Two men who had charge of the valuable freight thoughtlessly left the scattered goods at the bottom of the chasm and went to one of the huts to take something to eat before gathering up their master's goods. During their absence, fires were made to shed light on the wreck, which lay scattered in every direction, when a regular 'help yourselves, lads' took place. When the employees returned, flesh and bones of the half cow, the sheep and groceries had disappeared and there was not a witness to testify against the pilferers.''

The Sebastopol brickworks, a conspicuous feature of the area because of its two lanky chimneys, consisted of a large patent brick-making machine by Porter, Hind and Porter, of Carlisle, and extensive drying sheds. A never-ceasing ''traveller'' with a length of seventy yards, and operated in 1871 by two girls, delivered bricks to the shed above the ovens where they were dried by the waste heat. James Rixon, the manager, had a staff of twenty-six. Local shale and clay were mixed for the bricks.

The bed of clay, which lay under a thin strata of peat, contained much material of a sandy nature which could not be used. A crushing machine ground shale, which was then intermixed with the clay to make the bricks. Each oven had two fireholes and was was capable of holding from 14,000 to 15,000 bricks at a time. It took about a week to bake a consignment of bricks, the maximum daily output of the plant as a whole being from 18,000 to 20,000. Many of the bricks were transported to Blea Moor to line and arch the tunnel.

The glacial clay on the Moss was found to be comparatively free from limestone pebbles which would have caused bricks to shatter under heat. Ribblehead bricks were, none the less, poor in quality being apt to flake readily when exposed to inclement weather. Any defective bricks, such as those which fused during firing or contained stones, were dumped on a spoil heap.

The weather ruled. A freak storm on July 9, 1870 transformed what was normally a pleasant beck north of Blea Moor into a flood which burst the banks, sending an unstoppable torrent of water, and earth and stones roared into the heading of the tunnel. Five men were working in a heading which was ten feet wide and eight feet high, extending into the hill for forty yards. Three men escaped from the rushing water. The other two, Williams and Bell, were trapped but managed to climb into a tip wagon. The stupified Bell was heard mumbling what was almost certainly a prayer. Williams, standing on the front of the wagon, thrust his mouth as high as possible into an opening in the roof. He stood there, for two and a-half hours, with water at times entering his ears. The rescue party had to cope with the accumulated debris. Joseph Weston swam into the heading, with only fifteen inches of air space in which to breath, and located the dispirited Williams. A raft was floated in when the water allowed eighteen inches of roof space and so the brave Weston was able to rescue Williams. The other man had been drowned. His body, recovered with difficulty, was floated into the daylight on the raft.

In winter, the labour force was much reduced. Early in 1871, it was so cold that surface working was impossible. The disturbed boulder clay had frozen hard. By February, the fellsides were deep under snow. While the miners worked their twelve-hour shifts, six days a week, in the excavation of Blea Moor Tunnel, life elsewhere continued as best it could, under appalling conditions. When the weather moderated, there remained the problem of what to do with a legacy of the Ice Age, a porridge-like mush known as boulder clay, which in dry weather was hard as concrete and in wet conditions was like paste.

An engineer told F S Williams that when boulder clay was hard it must be drilled with holes and blasted with gun-powder. If rain fell, the thick gluey clay was ''so adhesive and tough that when the navvy sticks his pickaxe into it he can hardly get it out again, or if he does will not have loosened

PAY DAY AT BATTY GREEN

57

so much as a small teacupful of the stuff. Even when it has come out as dry rock and been put into the tip-wagon, a shower of rain, or even the jolting of a ride of a mile to the tip end, will perhaps shake the whole into a nearly semi-fluid mass of 'slurry', which settles down like glue to the bottom of the wagon and, when run to the tip-head, will drag the wagon over to the bottom of the embankment.'' This engineer had seen sixteen tip-wagons lying at one time at the bottom of the tip; ''and they would all have gone if we had to put on what we call a bulling-chain between the tip-raids which, the moment the wagon tipped its load, pulled up the wagon and prevented it from following.''

In February, 1871, a hard frost followed by a rapid thaw made excavations treacherous. There was a tolerable summer, during which many workmen left the hutments to assist on farms with haytime. In autumn, as they came trickling back, the wet weather re-established itself. Inside Blea Moor, the miners progressed at a mere 70 yards a month. More headings were arranged to speed up the work. In 1872, the partly-completed viaduct across Batty Moss dominated the scene and the first group of six on the northern side were made ready for arching. Every sixth pier was to be thicker than the others so that if one fell it would take only five other piers with it. In Blea Moor tunnel, about 300 miners, bricklayers and labourers worked by candlelight, the bill for candles alone being £50 a month.

Holes for the explosives were drilled by hand. Dynamite, then a novelty, costing £200 a ton (five times more than gunpowder) and having to be transported by road from Carlisle and Newcastle, was packed into them and ignited by means of a time fuse. A visitor who was shown some dynamite later said it had looked very much like potted lobster. ''It will not explode, we are told, unless heated to 420 deg.F. If a match is placed against it, the dynamite burns like fat or grease. The extra heat required to make it explode is obtained by a cap of 'fulminating powder'. Dynamite can be carried about and *is* carried about to bring it to the required temperature, if frozen, in one's trousers pocket, as it will not explode if exceedingly cold.''

Henry Wright, a 24-year-old miner, was in Blea Moor tunnel, cleaning out an old hole with a drill when he encountered some unspent dynamite. Severely wounded, he was taken to Batty Green Hospital, where he was attended by the company's doctor. Henry was transferred to Leeds Infirmary, where died a few days later. The body was brought back to Batty Green. After the inquest, held in the *Welcome Home Inn,* where a verdict of accidental death was recorded, a funeral procession started for Chapel-le-Dale.

The terrifying effect of a dynamite explosion was evident in February, 1875, when John Thompson disobeyed regulations and attempted to dry some dynamite at a brazier in Blea Moor Tunnel. Two workmen at a distance from Thompson, hearing an explosion, went to the spot, where they found the young miner's body dreadfully mangled and lifeless. They told the Coroner that the right side of his head, his face, and his right hand, were completely blown off, and the body was otherwise lacerated. ''The fragments of the body were carefully and sorrowfully gathered up and conveyed to the hospital at Batty Green. It was an appalling sight to see the torn-off fragments and the faceless head of a body still reeking with vitalised blood and not five minutes previously strong and healthy, and every way fitted for an active and useful life.'' A verdict of ''accident death'' was recorded and Thompson, aged 28, was buried in the extended yard of Chapel-le-Dale.

In February, 1875, the year when goods traffic was to begin on the Settle-Carlisle line, yet more workers died, one of them passing to the next world in sudden, dramatic circumstances. John Thompson, aged 28, was drying some dynamite over a fire in Blea Moor Tunnel when he was blown to pieces. The fragments of his body were ''carefully and sorrowfully gathered up'' and taken to Batty Green for the inquest. Henry Bachelor, aged 22, of Sebastopol, who was found dead on the Blea Moor stretch of the tramway, was known to be a heavy drinker. He had a scratch on his forehead, as though he had fallen heavily, and the inquest verdict was "found dead". Henry was the 210th person to be taken down to Chapel-le-Dale for burial. The extension to the churchyard was now almost full of the mortal remains of railway workers and their families.

In Blea Moor, black damp was met with in the headings. The men also reported an explosive stone (possibly they had struck an earlier charge which had failed to ignite). And when the way through was clear for a locomotive to reach the parties of miners, it did so noisily and smokily, "panting and spitting out fire, and filling the dark opening with rolls of foul and suffocating coal smoke." An ill-ventilated part of the tunnel had air so foul that men periodically stopped work and lay down "to breathe the lower stratum of air." An inspector reported that a workman was rendered so helpless through the obnoxious fumes that he had to be brought down from the heading to get his breath.

The debris from the headings was cleared away by labourers, much of it being taken to the bottom of a shaft, to be winched up in iron buckets. Material from the ends of the tunnel was removed by horse-drawn trolley. The horses were kept well-groomed and also bedecked with ribbons by their proud owners. James Sherman, the driver of a horse and cart, who had neglected to keep the tunnel well-lit, had one of his ankles crushed when he tripped and the wheel of a wagon passed over it. The accident was not considered serious, but James was weakened by loss of blood while being borne in an open cart over several miles of rough track to his lodgings at Batty Green. At one stage, blood was trickling from the cart. He refused medical aid and bled to death.

The summer of 1872 was one of the wettest on record, with 92 inches of rain recorded at Dent Head. The labour force slumped as men found more congenial work. Material needed for the embankments was too soft to be tipped so work in the cuttings stopped until the land hardened up again. Almost nine miles of permanent way, single line, had been laid between Settle Junction and the Ingleton road. Another half mile existed between here and the south face of the tunnel, which mean that wagons with coal and other material were now running from Settle to the summit of Blea Moor. It was timely, for coal which had been acquired from Ingleton Colliery in the old days at from fivepence or sixpence a load was now costing 1s.8d, with a prospect of a further rise. Six hundred tons of coal per month was used on Contract No 1 alone, there being ten locomotives and seventeen stationary engines at work continuously.

The engineers were proud of the 24-arch Batty Moss viaduct, draped across the dalehead with a length of 1,328 feet and a maximum height of 100 feet. The 45 ft spans had been assembled on wooden framing. When each frame had been removed, the arch was said to have dropped a mere quarter of an inch. The arches were covered with concrete, then overlaid with asphalt to deflect rainwater from the brickwork. The first train to cross the viaduct, on Sunday, September 6, 1874, was hauled by the locomotive *Diamond* (driven by J Pilgrim) and carried a stoker, guard and five passengers.

A navvy and his family enjoying a meal in one of the huts. Two main types of hut were in use, the large one having two bedrooms, one for the family and one for the lodgers.

Mr Tiplady's Mission

If any class of men have a right to say "No man cares for my soul", it is those men who make our great public iron highways...If churchmen and dissenters could join to save a drowning man, why not save a soul from hell and a multitude of sins?

Wesleyan local preacher (1872).

THE idea of a day school at Batty Green was broached in August, 1870, and it was opened in the springtime of 1871, when Miss Herbert of Nottingham had forty-three scholars who were reported to be clean, neatly attired "and on account of their docility and good behaviour a credit to their parents and the railway public." Children from other shanty towns did not attend this school because of the distance they must walk and also on account of the poor state of the road. A visitor in October, 1871, noted that "groups of children here and there were sitting on the moor, which must, on account of its swampy condition, be very injurious to their health. Surely the *Midland Company* might do something towards the education of those neglected children who through the circumstances of the workmen are deprived of the educational advantages of towns and villages."

The *Midland* and its Contractor, under the impulse of the Victorian "moral conscience", did what they could and also tried to divert the men's attention from "pursuits and places of a corrupting character". They did so by establishing railway mission stations, which were non sectarian. The missionary was essentially one with a loving heart and a desire to do the people good. Clergymen, if they wished, could appear in canonicals and read church prayers before the sermon.

James Tiplady was appointed by the Midland in collaboration with the Bradford City Mission as a Scripture Reader for Contract No 1. Tiplady's main base was a capacious Mission Room at Batty Green. The building was made available by William Ashwell, the *Midland's* representative on Contract No 1, who (wrote the Wesleyan preacher already mentioned) was always willing "to render help to anyone who is inclined to speak comfortable and encouraging words to the men on this portion of the line." In autumn, he opened a Reading Room "for the mental improvement and social entertainment" of the people. The library consisted of about 150 volumes. Five daily newspapers were taken, along with four weeklies and some useful periodicals.

The Mission Room was the focal point for evangelical witness as for Saturday Readings and the occasional concert. When the Room was opened, it was not quite finished, the forms to be provided as seating being incomplete. Chairs for the occasion were brought from the various huts. "As after this week, the railway missionary will have three mission rooms, and two day and two Sunday schools under his charge, it would be well if some large-hearted clergyman or lay preachers would pay the railway officials and workmen a visit and give them a sermon." Eventually, the Mission Room, also known as "the new chapel", had a platform for the minister and the singers. The forms were comfortable seats with backs and the place heated by two stoves. The plainness of the walls was off-set by "pictorial embellishment" intended to teach "the virtues of thrift, kindness, bearing, etc."

Young Mr Tiplady was stated, shortly after he arrived, to "labour assiduously". One of his sad tasks was to officiate at funerals. When Annie Wall, a girl newly arrived at Ribblehead, died through an accident while travelling with her aunt on a tramway train which became derailed, it was he who gave an oration at a funeral service in the family hut at Sebastopol and he accompanied the mourners when the body was borne in a small cart to the yard at Chapel-le-Dale. When Tiplady had been at Ribblehead for a year he was being described as "the pushing railway missionary". The emissary of the Church of England was the Rev W (William) M Harper, of Chapel-le-Dale, "a gentleman of genial spirit". He preached his farewell sermon at the little church in May, 1871.

Meekness was not one of the virtues of another Anglican clergyman, the Rev R Denny, Vicar of Ingleton, who presided over the local Bench and had little mercy on those navvies who strayed from the paths of righteousness. Richard Rogers, who slew a grouse on moorland belonging to James Farrer, was fined 20s and 14s costs. When the money was not forthcoming, Rogers went to gaol for a month, a high price for a single grouse. Down to the House of Correction at Wakefield went George Thompson and James Booth, two navvies who when drunk had stoned a policeman.

In what a writer described as "the half-savage world of the navvy" the civilising influences included weekly Penny Readings, gatherings which featured songs as well as recitations, covering the gamut of emotion, from sadness to elation, tears to laughter. The size of the audience was related to the weather and proceeds went to some "worthy cause", such as Leeds Infirmary. A grand entertainment took place at the Mission on March 13th, 1871. Around a hundred people sat down for tea. Visitors included Mr Whitehead (elocutionist), from Burnley, and some auditors from "fair London town". Mr Carr recited The Deceitful Lover and Watering Milk, or Choking the Best Cow. Miss Ellis sang The Ladder Style. Etc. There was an alternation of words spoken or sung. The entertainment ended at almost 10pm.

The Rev William Harper, whose signature was added to numerous entries in the register of deaths at Chapel-le-Dale, left the area at a time when smallpox was painfully prevalent in some of the huts at Sebastopol and Jericho. A mother and her three children died of "the infectious malady". In one week, Harper's successor, the Rev E Smith, officiated when five smallpox victims were interred and a request was made to the *Midland* for financial help in enlarging the burial ground. (The company granted £20 and the extension was consecrated in August).

When Miles Tailford Hall, of Batty Wife Hole, died from smallpox after only four days illness, his body was laid to rest in an independent burial ground at Dent, with Mr Tiplady and the Independent Minister officiating. In 1871, Tiplady was regularly attending a wooden "mission station" at Dent Head. Clergymen and lay preachers were encouraged to take services there. Early in 1872, a wooden building was erected at the southern end of Blea Moor tunnel to serve as a Reading Room and School in an area somewhat remote from Batty Green.

On a crisp winter Sunday, Mr Ashwell the Contractor made one of the engines available to Tiplady and a visiting preacher so that they might visit the higher camps. The drive took them via Jericho to Tunnel Huts. "The engine driver had to check his iron steed again and again, when some youth mounted the engine to receive a *British Workman,* a portion of the New Testament or some other work from the hands of the missionary. Mr Tiplady is well supplied by the Company with useful and starling periodicals, so that he can supply them with a generous hand to young or old if they have any taste for reading." At Jericho, the two men wandered among the huts, with the visitor impressed by "the large number of healthy-looking children, who were neatly clothed and evidently, from their merry and ruddy countenances, were well-fed. Hitherto, the children at Jericho and the Tunnel Huts had no school privileges and their parents no place of worship to attend within a reasonable distance.

"In one of the huts so many workmen were sitting together that after Mr Tiplady had left, the visitor addressed a few homely and friendly words on doing well for themselves for both time and eternity...The men were remarkably civil." In

Page 30.

BURIALS in the Parish of *Chapel le Dale or Ingleton Fells*
in the County of *York* in the Year 18_71_

Name.	Abode.	When buried.	Age.	By whom the Ceremony was performed.
William Dean No. 233.	Sebastopool	Jan. 22	11 months	Wm Harper
John Hollerenshaw No. 234.	Sebastopool	Jan. 24	40 years	Wm Harper
Charles Bibby No. 235.	Sebastopool	Jan. 31	9 months	Wm Harper
Louisa Annie Thompson No. 236.	Jericho	Feb. 1	3 years	Wm Harper
Fredrick Little No. 237.	Inkerman	Feb. 5	4 years	Wm Harper
Tom Atkinson Little No. 238.	Inkerman	Feb. 9	1 year & six month	Wm Harper
Thomas Smith No. 239.	Jericho	Feb. 12	10 months	Wm Harper
Ellen Higgins No. 240.	Blaemoor	March 26	1 year & 7 months	Wm Harper

another hut, some of the men were reading. An Irishman had the *Common Prayer Book* in his hands. "He is a common workmen with a large family in Ireland and still I was told that he is in the habit of sending a sovereign weekly to his family. When asked how he managed to do it, to his honour and good sense he said that he could not think of spending his money on drink and let his wife and children at home be in want. If reading the *Prayer Book* on Sunday on a barren moor, when a man is cut off from a place of worship, leads a man to thus remember his distant family, it would be well if more of the railway operatives would go and do likewise." After leaving the huts, the two preachers climbed to the summit of Blea Moor on a pathway which at times was plated with ice. The fells were covered with snow and bright with sunlight. "It was a sight to make one forget tired limbs." And on they went to Dent Head.

For the opening meeting of the Reading Room and School at Jericho, an event which was advertised as a tea and entertainment, a locomotive and wagon started from Batty Green station at about 5pm. Beside the driver and stoker on the engine, and in the wagon, were many passengers, plus a harmonium, a barrel of cookery, abundance of bread, sweet and plain, a number of forms "and other articles too numerous to mention". The locomotive's approach to Blea Moor was through a deep cutting and over frail wooden bridges. The engine stopped at the missionary hut. The noises and sights were bewildering to the Mission folk. Lads and men were running up and down with lighted lamps or gathering round the engine. Up on the Moor lights were flaring and the clang of machinery sounded from the tunnel shafts. Men shouted instructions as with the engine they started on their return journey.

When all had been comfortably arranged in the new building, tea was served. "After the table had been cleared, a pretty large company assembled to listen to the readings and songs of the evening. The first reading was John

Ploughman's Home, delivered by Mr Tiplady. A workman who carries a hurdy-gurdy about with him being in the room, and asked to give the audience a tune, he played a polka, which had an exciting influence upon some of the women who could not keep their feet still. "The Disaster at Batty Green" was recited by Mr Burgoin. It related to an incident which must have occurred to a "smart young grocer" called William White who put a horse into the shafts of a cart. The horse took fright and man, horse and cart fell into "that awful precipice which is known as Batty's Hole". Five strong men moved the cart. The horse and driver were in the water, he sitting trembling on the horse's head. The rescue was successful, though some provisions were lost. Another man offered to drive the cart to Dent, but half a mile down the road the horse was again troublesome.

It stopped abruptly and the contents of the cart, including several men, were tipped on to the ground.

> A potato now it marks the spot
> Upon yon lonely moor,
> Where Messrs C----, T and B.,
> Were thrown upon the floor.

There were more items at the concert. Then the hurdy-gurdy was again brought into play, "when its magic strains again excited more powerfully the dancing spirit into the younger part of the audience."

In February, 1872, James Tiplady married a Bradford woman and transferred to the *Midland* line near Chesterfield. The *Lancaster Guardian* correspondent noted: "As Mr Tiplady was wearied with his lonely position, he a few days ago bid farewell to bachelordom at Bradford, and in consequence of the delightful step he had taken, his friends at Batty Green resolved to furnish him with some useful domestic article as a token of their high esteem." The event took place in the Mission Room. Job Hirst, sub-contractor on the viaduct, presided and an address was delivered by Tiplady's successor, Henry Hancock. A cruet stand was presented to the departing missionary by William Burgoin and was accompanied by a testimonial, headed "Ingleton-road, near Ingleton, Feb 29th, 1872".

The message reflected the fulsome manner of the Victorian period: "The small memento with which this address is accompanied is an expression of the kindly feeling entertained by a few of the residents at Batty Green, and is not merely intended as a souvenir of the event which has so recently taken place, but is also an acknowledgement of his arduous and successful labours as a missionary in this neighbourhood." The Batty Greeners also wished Mr and Mrs Tiplady "many years of happy union on earth, hoping that they might share largely in the good opinion of all who knew them now and who may know them thereafter. Etc."

On a Sunday in August, two devout men—a Methodist local preacher and Mr Hancock, the new railway missionary—visited Blea Moor with the object of preaching in the open air. They approached from the north, via Newby Head and Dent Head, using a horse and trap provided by William Ashwell. At Dent Head, beside the viaduct, was the Mission House, serviced by Wesleyans from Dent and Sedbergh. The visiting preachers had an impromptu service, with many of the workmen standing around in their shirt sleeves, some smoking, one holding a cat and another a dog. "Not a word would the writer use to cast a slight on those men, for it was quite a pleasure to minister to their spiritual wants and to see their behaviour so good. Though Saturday night was pay night, it was pleasant to see that none of them was under the influence of drink." The visitors were entertained to a good meal.

They now began the return trip over Blea Moor to Batty Green. At the Tunnel Huts, in contrast with Dent Head, there was much drunkenness. "We distributed a few tracts and spoke a few friendly words to the men, who were very civil. If a navvy should chance to show a little rudeness, he would soon be checked by his mates. They heard that the day school was being well attended. "No one can pass over these railway works without remarking on the great number of children." At Jericho, "many of the men were under the influence of drink but they treated us with much respect. A number of men were playing at pitch and toss, but as soon as we began singing they ceased and came and listened very attentively. One young man who had drunk deep was rather noisy at times but he had no ill in him. Many of the men checked him again and again for his talking propensity."

The congregation numbered about seventy. When prison life was mentioned, one of the men said: "I've just come from a month of it." Another remarked the service was the happiest hour he had spent for three years. And, as at Dent Head, they were provided with food, many of the railway families being willing to entertain the preachers.

Scripture Readers on Contract No 1 left the employ of the *Midland* during the summer of 1875. They were given three months' notice and a gratuity of £10. The Mission Hall at Batty Green was converted into two huts. What had Mr Tiplady and Mr Hancock (and their brethren on other Contracts) achieved? A reflective note, in the *Lancaster Guardian* for July 4, 1874, observed that "as a rule all Christian teaching will fail unless the missionary be of a friendly and gentlemanly disposition, and will take a pleasure in visiting them (the navvies) in the huts." This was done as time allowed.

Like John Wesley, they invariably preached in the open air. A newspaper writer affirmed: "Parsons who can only preach to respectable congregations in churches and chapels are not the class of teachers to reach the navvies."

Rather more than two hundred interments took place at Chapel-le-Dale churchyard, which was extended to meet the demand for space. When a curate forgot to arrange a funeral, so that no grave was dug, the navvy himself dug it and laid in it the bodies of his two children. Fellow workmen and the Midland Railway Company paid for a marble plaque commemorating those who died. It was affixed to a wall inside the church.

Bad Lads and Lasses

Let the navvy work where he may, he must have his ale, and brewers, spirit merchants, licensed victuallers and unlicensed innkeepers, are always ready to supply him with his favourite drink.

A Newspaper Correspondent, 1874.

INGLETON Fair, held in November, was renowned for the amount of ale which flowed. One might suppose that navvies were among the crowd in 1874, when "there was a good deal of drinking and it was with a little difficulty that the rain and the police cleared the streets." Drinking was maintained on the following day, when the Sports took place in a field behind the *Wheatsheaf* inn.

The "thin blue line" was headed by William Exton, Superintendent of Police for the Ewecross Division, who was based at Ingleton. He had a daily reminder, by traffic going to and from the railway station, of the feverish railway activity at the dalehead. His Sergeants were William Clapham, at Ingleton, and Thomas Inman, based at Sedbergh. Of the Constables, the two most concerned with the Ribblehead shanties were Archie Cameron, stationed at Batty Green, and John Otter Taylor at Dent Head. A police presence was maintained under the terms of John Ashwell's contract.

Archie Cameron, of whom nothing is known except his name, travelled to Ingleton on Court days, for it is more than likely that someone from the shanties was appearing before the Bench, which in those undemocratic times consisted of the local gentry and parsons. There were occasions when plain clothes were in order, such as when a policeman at Settle observed and then apprehended three railway labourers who were playing at pitch and toss on the New Road on the Sabbath. Taken to Court, the men were cautioned by the Rev H J Swale and then discharged. "It is hoped," he said, doubtless in his most sonorous parsonical voice, "that this will have the desired effect of preventing this Sunday gambling."

As early as 1870, the police in north-west Yorkshire were able to make use of a national telegraph system. A Swansea woman, anxious about the whereabouts of her husband, Edward Town, a sub-contractor on the railway, contacted the police at Settle by telegram. They forwarded the inquiry to Ingleton, from where instructions were sent at a late hour on the Sabbath to PC Goodison, stationed at Gearstones, near Ribblehead. The constable waited for the fading of the last moments of the Sabbath before pouncing on his unsuspecting prey - fast asleep in a house at Horton-in-Ribblesdale with a bigamous wife. Town was taken to the lock-up at Ingleton. The details were transmitted by telegram to Swansea, and back by wire came instructions that Town should be taken to Lancaster, where Mr Superintendent Allison would be waiting. The second Mrs Town, clinging tearfully to her "husband" until the last moment, said she would remain faithful to him.

In June, 1873, an embezzler by the name of Charles Harris, aged 32 years, was apprehended at Selside by PC Walker. It was revealed that the prisoner, a Bedfordshire man, had been employed as a trolley man on the *Midland Railway*. As he had belonged to the Bedfordshire Militia, he had been undergoing military training. After committing the offence, he was traced to Leicester, where he stayed a few days. Harris was then located at Selside, near Ribblehead. A warrant for his arrest was issued and he was taken to the lock-up at Ingleton. "At 5pm the same day, a telegraphic message was sent to Mr George, Head Constable, Dunstable, that Harris was in the policeman's hands. Three hours later, a message was received from Mr George that an officer would arrive the next day to collect the prisoner." Mr George himself arrived by train on the *London and North-Western line.* He took the prisoner away by the *Midland* express train at 3-20pm.

Theft, though the commonest form of law-breaking, was usually of the petty variety. George Morris stole three items, including a jack plane and a smoothing plane belonging to George Steddon, who worked by Messrs Burgoin and Cocks at Batty Green. Morris was picked up when, travelling down the dale towards Settle, pursued by Messrs Steddon and Burgoin in the grocer's horse and trap, he did the Victorian equivalent of "thumbing a lift". The men in the trap being glad to oblige promptly turned the trap round and drove back to Batty Green, where George Morris was handed over to the police. Brought before the magistrates at Ingleton, he pleaded guilty to three charges of theft and the sentence was a month's imprisonment for each offence.

In the summer of 1871, John Cockshott (alias Como) was brought to heel for stealing a £5 note of the type issued by the Craven Bank. In this case, it had become the property of the *Midland Railway Company.* Not often did a navvy show remorse for wrong-doing though in a case where James Jackson was "sent down" for three months for theft, the Court reporter noticed that his eyes "glistened with tears".

In the case of violent death at the shanties, the Coroner or his deputy travelled by horse and trap to a venue at Batty Green. An inquest was usually held in the *Welcome Home* inn, one of two temporary hostelries, the other being the *Railway.* Drink befuddled the navvy mind. There was plenty of it, for Batty Green had its own brewery, the hostelries did well and a man might buy ale (or something stronger) at one of the huts, where it was offered without the blessing of the Revenue authorities. The Settle Temperance Society held meetings to denounce Demon Drink. At the close of a meeting at Batty Green, there might be twenty men signing the pledge. Others, having weighed up the pro's and cons, later signed the pledge in the presence of Mr Tiplady.

A diversion on many a Saturday night or early Sunday morning was a bare-fisted fight. In 1870, one of the combatants was so drunk it was decided to postpone the battle until 5-30am on Sunday. Another time, a boxer stopped and went to bed, had a sound sleep and rose to resume the fight. William Williams (alias Nobby Scandalous) and John Atkins (Policeman Jack) fought on the road one Sunday morning. Both men fell and Williams suffered injuries from which he died. At the inquest, which Atkins did not attend, having absconded, it was said that the fight lasted for a quarter of an hour. The two men had been sober. They fought with their fists and had not kicked each other.

Not many women featured in Court proceedings, but Mary Ann Lee, a native of Milnthorpe who was also a widow, aged 32 years, pleaded guilty to charges of drunkenness and indecent exposing of her person. The charge against her was laid under the Refreshment Houses Act, 23 Victoria, chap 27 and sec 40. The magistrates were told that her shameless and nameless indecencies had made her "one of the lowest and most polluted of womankind." Police Sergeant Wildman told the magistrates how he apprehended her. Following up many complaints, he visited the *Hill Inn*, Chapel-le-Dale, and found her dancing in an indecent manner with drunken navvies. The landlord having had his attention drawn to a breach of the law, directed Mary Lee to the door. She behaved so badly, she was taken to the Ingleton lock-up. The Rev R Denny, who presided over the Bench, told her she was a disgrace to decent society. He hoped she would amend her ways. She was fined 40s and costs (9s.6d). In default, there would be two months' imprisonment. No money was forthcoming. Mary Lee went to gaol.

Mrs Overman, of Sebastopol, who kept a grocer's shop at Batty Green for Messrs Burgoin and Cocks, charged Mrs Emmerton, one of her neighbours, with common assault upon her. The quarrel was caused through the plaintiff's desire to have the defendant's hut removed. It seems that

Mrs Emmerton and her husband, visiting the plaintiff's shop, called her "names not fit to be repeated". About 2pm, on the same day, Mrs Emmerton returned and the quarrel rumbled on. For the defence, Ann Simpson said that on coming out of her door when she heard a noise she saw all the parties were quarrelling. Mrs Overton struck the defendant first and before the defendant pulled her hair off. The case was dismissed.

In October, 1871, when the Batty Green Sports took place at the *Viaduct Inn*, a number of women settled their differences using their firsts. Wife-beating was not uncommon in Victorian days. One of the wife-beaters was John Parker, the Batty Green chimney sweep, who in 1871 was bound over in £10 surety for threatening to do bodily injury to his wife. To be fair, he had been provoked. At the same Court, a twenty-four year old railway labourer called William Tomlinson received two months hard labour, having been found under Mrs Parker's bed.

Some cases of lawlessness were exceedingly complex. In February, 1871, James Rixon, head of the Sebastopol brickworks, was arrested for using threatening language to Henry White and a warrant was issued for his arrest. Rixon's manner was understandable when it was heard that White had abducted his wife and fled to Ingleton, where they had taken the 10-10 to Skipton, staying at an inn as man and wife. The wife went off to Leeds. White returned to Ingleton, where he was pursued around the district by Rixon and PC Goodison. At Batty Green, the policeman was asked to go to Nixon's house to check goods stolen by the wife. Some men were present. White lay injured on a sofa. Rixon threatened White with a gun. Most people sympathised with him—until he was apprehended for assaulting Emma Shackleton, following a dispute between Emma's husband and Rixon about sub-money to the value of five shillings. Emma, having reproved Rixon for striking a bystander in the crowd, was hit in the face.

The ale can was the cause of much of the disorder. The *Lancaster Guardian,* in 1871, considered that the riotous conduct of men quartered on Blea Moor was ''the shame and bane of Christian Britain'', adding: ''Drink appears to be such a necessary in the dietary of a navvy that whether working or playing, with money or without it, he must have drink. If his money be done before his thirst for drink is slaked, he will sell jacket, shoes, braces or any article of clothing he can dispense with, to get his favourite beverage. When clothes and credit are gone, as a last resource he will in piteous terms appeal to mates or strangers, either for pence or a drink of their pot of beer.''

When, in the summer of 1871, Mr Ashwell ordered that six barrels of beer should be confiscated and stove in, the workers—in a case of tit for tat—waylaid some wiskey (sic) from a man who was collecting some of the liquor from a pub on behalf of Mr Ashwell. One of the men declared that if whisky was not to have a lodging place at the huts, he and his friends did not consider it contrary to Mr Ashwell's orders to transfer it to their stomachs!

Fights, induced by heavy drinking, were commonplace. Those who did not drink regularly wondered if the Ingleton magistrates were right to give the railway workmen so many facilities for getting drunk. Few of those who applied for permission to sell beer and spirits were refused. Batty Green's two pubs and the brewery stood near the office at which the workmen were paid. From the *Railway Inn* at Batty Green, one dark evening, stumbled Peter Miles, a thirty-year-old mason and native of Bootle, near Liverpool. He wandered on to the tramway, where it is supposed to lay down and fell asleep. Two hours later, at 10-15pm, he was crushed to death by a locomotive. Henry Bailey, the guard, told the Coroner he was returning from Jericho when, at about 150 yards from Batty Green platform, he felt a jerk and ordered the driver to apply the brakes. Bailey had alighted to find the body of Miles, whose skull had been cut through and his abdomen sadly mutilated. The verdict was "accidentally killed".

No "watering hole" was better known than the *Welcome Home,* where the welcome was afforded by James Mathers. There was general sadness, in May, 1872, when news of his death through an accident at Ingleton reached Ribblehead. He had gone to Ingleton with a horse and cart. When the horse bolted, he attempted to grab the harness, slipped and was killed when a wagon wheel passed over his neck. The inquest verdict was "accidental death" and Mathers was buried in Chapel-le-Dale, where in course of time a substantial tombstone was erected to his memory. Mrs Mathers, "a kind-hearted soul", who was left with the care of a small daughter, kept the business running.

A haven for drunken men who were locked out of their lodgings was (as mentioned) the engine shed at the southern end of Blea Moor tunnel. To this shed, a little before midnight, in the summer of 1871, staggered Thomas Jones (alias Wesh Nobby), a labourer and veteran of various railway projects. He and another man, being well and truly drunk, were seen linking arms to hold each other up. Jones's affairs were discussed at the Court House in Ingleton, where he was charged with robbing the shop window of John Clark Garlic, innkeeper and grocer of Batty Wife. Jones was said by Edwin Farmer, mason of Jericho, to have visited the public house where he lodged. He had begun drinking about 5-20pm and stayed until between 11pm and midnight. Jones returned to the public house early on the following day. What had happened to him in the meantime was revealed by Matthew Frost, an engine driver. Jones had stopped in the engine shed until after daybreak, three or four o'clock. He was carrying a dinner handkerchief in which reposed something bulky. James Shepherd testified that the drinking was resumed before Jones went off to work again. He had demanded a quart of ale. Thomas Jones claimed he had bought the objects from a tramp. The magistrates did not believe him.

It was not uncommon for police and excise officers to sneak

up on huts and look through windows, waiting for ale to be supplied and payment made before moving in to make an arrest of the person, usually a woman, who had been selling ale or "malt, spirituous and other liquors" without a licence. Joseph Wilson, an excise officer living at Bentham, who called at the hut for some beer, gave the defendant a shilling and received the appropriate amount of change. The Licensing Acts had been violated. The law took its course.

During the hot summer of 1871, workers inflamed by drink were inclined to damage property—or themselves. In early August, at Ingleton Court, fines were imposed on George and Joseph Laydall, Thomas Rogers, W Leason and George Davis, were brickmakers of Sebastopol, who in the course of a binge at the *Welcome Home* smashed eight squares of glass, two window frames and six gill glasses. The fines were 5s each, with 9s costs and £2 towards the damage.

The most celebrated story of a railway labourer acting violently while "under the influence of drink" took place at *Gearstones* in May,1873. George Young, a railway labourer, threw some dynamite on to the fire and caused considerable damage to the building, also injuring a few customers. The kettle which had been standing in front of the fire was blown to pieces, and some fragments were produced in evidence when, at Ingleton Court on the following day, Young was charged with doing serious damage. Alice Yates, daughter of Francis Yates, the inn-keeper, said that the prisoner arrived in the front kitchen of the inn between 4pm and 5pm and called for some drink. About 6pm, she saw him with a tin box in his hand and what looked like gun caps, but were longer. Young said he would not strike one of them for a sovereign for if he did it would blow up the house. About 7pm, Alice heard a loud report. The house appeared to shake and she thought it was about to collapse. The kitchen and lobby were so full of smoke that for some time she could not see anyone.

At the time of the explosion, there were thirteen people in the house and seven in the kitchen, where the prisoner was drinking. Alice, entered the kitchen as Young was emerging, pushed him back and said: "Oh, you bad man. What have you done?" He did not admit to doing anything. Yet the explosion had blown the oven and fireplace grate from their places. The front of the boiler was shattered and the kitchen badly damaged. Fifteen paines of glass had been shattered and part of a window frame was broken. The kitchen clock was destroyed. In the back kitchen, the oven was lifted from its place and the partition between kitchen and house was holed. The room above the front kitchen had its hearthstone lifted out of place. The glass in a funeral card was broken. The ceiling of an adjoining bedroom was cracked.

John Butcher, a navvy on tramp, was present about 7pm when George Young took something like an ounce of tobacco, rolled it up and threw it at a man nicknamed Cheshire, who tossed it back. Young then produced from his pocket the tin box already referred to and he took an object from it, putting it in the parcel which he had thought held tobacco. At the time, Young was standing by the fire. He then tossed the parcel into the fire. There was an immediate explosion, a flash of fire striking the witness on the side of his head and on one of his legs. Soon afterwards, Butcher followed Young into the road, collared him and knocked him down. He then dragged him into the inn, where he stood guard over him until the arrival of PC Cameron.

Another witness, George Wright, appeared at Court with his head bandaged, his face swollen and severely burnt. Nothing was visible but the tip of his nose and his eyes and mouth. His badly injured right hand was in a sling and his left hand was bandaged. Wright testified that he had been visiting Batty Green and was on his way back to his hut at Denthead when he decided to call at *Gearstones* for a drink. He arrived at about 7pm and saw Young throw something in the fire. There was an explosion and he was badly injured, a doctor having dressed his wounds on the following morning.

The more athletic and wily navvies poached Mr Farrer's

grouse from the moor and trout from Gayle Beck, Cam Beck or the Ribble. In 1872, James Farrer retired from hearing a case of poaching trout heard at Ingleton because of his involvement as owner of the fishery. The poachers, James Simpson and Samuel Gilibrand, were scouring Cam Beck one Sunday when they were apprehended by Robert Staveley, the game-watcher. Simpson protested his innocence. No fish had been caught. In any case, the men had been at the water for only about four minutes. Fines were imposed.

The methods used by Settle-Carlisle navvies when fishing were not those recommended by the gentry. Pools were dynamited or lime added to the water to remove the oxygen. The old blacksmith's trick of hitting likely stones in the river with a sledge hammer and stunning any fish which had taken sanctuary there was practised. The grappling technique of drawing a barbed hook across the river and snagging any luckless fish was also evident.

The law was inclined to over-react to a situation which might at any time become explosive. Robert Wright, "an elderly looking railway labourer of between fifty and sixty years of age" got drunk on Sports Day and made a wild statement which landed him in court at Ingleton, charged with attempting to commit suicide by cutting his throat. It was recognised that the charge was more serious than the incident. On this occasion at least, justice was tempered with mercy. The old chap went free.

Sickness and Death

It is singular that in a mountainous district, so remote from the great centres of industry, men, women and children from every county in England, as well as Wales, Scotland and Ireland, should be buried in a quiet chur-chyard which few of them had heard of before they came into the district.

Note about Chapel-le-Dale, 1875.

MONEY for medical care came in part from the Settle and Carlisle Sick Fund, which was established among the workpeople towards the end of 1870. Three years later, the membership was 140. A shortfall in funds was met by organising an entertainment in the Settle Music Hall, over £10 being raised. At Ribblehead, John Ashwell, the Contractor, had a simple wooden building erected as a hospital. When Ashwell was in financial dif-ficulties, and the *Midland* took over the Contract, they also accepted responsibility for the hospital and appointed their own doctor. Those in need at the hutment of Denthead were attended by Dr Swain of Sedbergh.

Doctors were not themselves immune from misfortune. In the summer of 1871, during a thunderstorm, Dr Griffiths set off from Batty Green to Ingleton, where his professional ser-vices were needed. A young man had been thrown from a horse, injuring his head. The doctor's horse, startled by a flash of lightning, reared up, the rider being thrown to the ground. He was able to remount and the journey was resumed.

The first horse-drawn ambulance at Batty Green resembled one of the "covered wagons" made famous by their use on the plains of the American West. The Yorkshire type of wagon took patients to a temporary wooden hospital, though in some cases of serious injury, a workman was bundled on to the back of a handy cart and taken to his quarters at one of the settlements. In the few recorded cases where this happened, the patients died, usually from loss of blood.

When, in May 1871, the viral disease of smallpox broke out in the shanties of Sebastopol and Jericho, the Batty Green hospital was enlarged to deal with victims. Edwin S Green, Medical Officer of the Temporary Smallpox and Fever Hospital at Batty Green, writing on July 10, 1871 in response to a critical letter from a reader with the pen-name of Minimus, indicated that as soon as smallpox showed itself Mr Ashwell, the contractor, made an offer to the Board of Guardians of the Settle Union to erect at his own expense two detached buildings of the ordinary hut size for up to ten smallpox patients. The Guardians would fit it up (with the exception of beds) and maintain it at their own expense.

For almost three months, the threat of smallpox held everyone's attention. By the end of August, only three patients were left in hospital and an assistant nurse was made redundant. A dread of catching the disease reduced the number of visitors to the railway works, though a young lady from Settle, one of a mixed party, clambered into a locomotive and was taken on the tramway to Blea Moor where, properly attired, she descended in succession the three shafts of the tunnel.

The Smallpox Year of 1871 ended with a "strange scene" in the graveyard at Chapel-le-Dale, when the twin daughters of a miner living with his family at the Tunnel Huts were interred. The twins lived for a few days. Notice was given to the curate in charge of the parish during the absence of the Vicar that the funeral would take place on December 6th. On the 4th, at about 5pm, the father told the clergyman the interment would take place on another day at 2pm.

The funeral cortege, arriving about five minutes before the

time mentioned, found the gates to the Churchyard were locked. No bell was being tolled, as was customary. And neither the curate nor the sexton was present. After some delay, the curate appeared and, "with vexing nonchalance", told the bereaved parent that he had forgotten all about the funeral and consequently he had not notified the sexton about making a grave. The father of the dead children borrowed tools, dug a grave, tolled the bell and then filled in the grave which his own hands had dug. As a newspaper writer put it: "May such a painful scene never be witnessed in an English churchyard again."

The church which gave its name to Chapel-le-Dale had for long attracted attention because of its pretty situation and a description of it given by Southey in his novel *The Doctor*. The vicar, the Rev E Smith, with the co-operation of his parishioners, improved the environs of the chapel and now there was a lych gate at the entrance. Mr Smith spent £16 of his own money on evergreens and clinging roses. Just across the beck, in its own grounds, stood a big new vicarage.

In 1871, a visitor "could not but notice how the green mounds, which marked the resting places of the dead, had increased since the beginning of the Settle-Carlisle Railway. At the east end of the chapel yard, twenty-six green mounds contain the mouldering dust of adults and children from the railway works." At the west end were four graves, "making the number to thirty of those who have departed this life within seven months." Everyone who died received a decent burial. "In numerous cases," wrote a local correspondent, "young men have left the homes of their youth, and then, after leading a wandering life, have died far from the place of their birth, to find their last resting place amongst strangers. Though such men are often buried unattended by any of their relatives, still there are always sympathisers who will gather round their graves and shed a tear over their fallen mates."

The churchyard extension, which was necessary "on account of the terrible havoc made amongst the inhabitants at the new railway works on Blea Moor by the smallpox'', was consecrated on August 12, 1871. Over thirty people who had died of smallpox lay in the old burial ground. A contemporary account noted: ''Upon an average, before the railway works were commenced, there were about two interments per year. The old burial ground measured thirty-two perches and the new twenty-four perches. Earl Bective has kindly given the new ground. To unite both portions of ground, the old road to the farms which lie at the foot of Whernside has been broken up and a new and better road made. All the farmers who travelled over the road to their farmsteads, like sensible men, gave their willing consent to the alteration.

''Monday last being the day appointed for consecrating the new ground, Dr Ryan, Vicar of Bradford, and lately a colonial bishop, attended in place of the Bishop of Ripon to perform the rite of consecration. As the day was remarkably fine, the farmers in the locality were too busy with their haymaking to attend the service in the chapel. A few strangers from a distance were present. The prayers were read by the Rev E Smith, Vicar of Chapel-le-Dale. The first lesson, the 23rd ch. of Genesis, was read by the Rev Canon Marriner, of Clapham. This portion of holy writ, which spoke of the death of Sarah in her 128th year, and of the proper concern Abraham manifested to secure a burial place for his dead, was very appropriate for the occasion. The 2nd lesson, which was a portion of the Gospel of St John, was read by the Rev R Denny, Vicar of Ingleton. The sermon, which was founded on the 12th verse of the 90th Psalm, was a homely and excellent discourse, well adapted to the occasion and to a country congregation.''

The railway workers usually showed great sympathy towards one another in sickness or death. A visitor who observed the funeral of a young man, with the coffin placed in a wagon and drawn slowly by a locomotive on the tramway to Batty Green, commented that ''the attendants were numerous and respectably dressed.'' Less commendable was the manner of people at a funeral which took place on March 26, 1871. There was an interlude, as the body of a child was borne from Blea Moor huts to the church, when the bearers stopped at the *Hill Inn* for a drink, leaving the coffin on the road. Job Hirst, sub-contractor of the Batty Moss viaduct, died on December 7th, 1873. A committee of workmen and others arranged for a tombstone to be erected over his grave, which was dug just inside the Churchyard, to the right of the lych gate. The memorial stone, for which subscriptions amounting to £43.1s.5d had been raised, was put in place on the 23rd.

Money raised at concerts bought a memorial plaque for Chapel-le-Dale church in remembrance of those who had lost their lives by accident on the Settle-Carlisle (Contract No 1). One such concert was give in the schoolroom at Batty Green by a group from Settle who opened their programme with a glee, Huntsman's Chorus, and ended with a quartet, Ye Banks and Braes, by Misses Nelson and Hardacre, Messrs Overing and Hamilton. The expenses incurred when organising a second concert was defrayed by Messrs Burgoin and Cocks. "The room was densely packed. Afterwards, a ball was given, which was kept up with high glee until 6am. Among those present were Dr and Mrs Dobbie, of Batty Green."

In March, 1874, the Rev R Denny (Vicar of Ingleton and a stern Chairman of the local bench of magistrates) preached his farewell sermon, to an overflowing congregation. Having been minister of Ingleton parish for twenty-eight years, he was leaving for a new home at Tatham Rectory.

In 1874, the Settle Board of Guardians, having considered that the hospital at Batty Green was of no further use, decided to sell it. Before an advertisement was devised, three men visited the hospital to measure it up. They entered the deadhouse and one of them, seeing a coffin, exclaimed: "There's a man in it!" Another man said they must have forgotten to bury him. "No, he has his clothes on," said the one who had lifted the lid. When that lid was again raised, it was found that the man's trousers were stained with blood. Had he been murdered? And had the murderer brought his victim to the dead-house by night and dumped him in the remaining coffin? The visitors held a consultation and decided that the Coroner must be informed. A contemporary account relates that all this time the man was lying in the coffin with his face downwards, and to all appearance, the stillness was that of death. A third gentleman approached the coffin to examine the murder victim and ascertain whether death had been recent or not. He was pinching the man's leg to assess whether it was rigid or flabby when the "corpse" raised his head and gruffly said: "Can't you let a poor fellow sleep quietly?" He began to yawn and rub his eyes.

It was a navvy, sleeping off the "stupifying influence of alcohol" and not particular about which bed he chose. Though this navvy was still drunk, he asked for threepence so that he might buy another pint of beer. The coffin in which the navvy was found had been sprinkled with sawdust and used for the corpses of those who had died in smallpox or from fevers, until proper coffins could be made.

This navvy, ignoring the risks to his health (or to any others he might contact) left Batty Green with the intention of going to Keighley.

On to Completion

Now that the heavy work has been got over, all concerned may fairly be congratulated upon the substantial and thorough style in which it has been done.
Lancaster Guardian, May, 1875.

T HE year 1874 dawned with grim weather, both rain and snow. The tedium of life in a remote area led to more alcoholism in the hutments. Most of the liquor consumed had not received the blessing of the Excise, and one of its officers, visiting Blea Moor, was served with a drink illegally. Mary Ann Turner, whose hut it was, was brought before the magistrates at Ingleton, who fined her.

May was not a merry month. The fells were snow-covered. In one week, the railway folk experienced frost and snow, hail and rain, and a few calm periods between days when the wind howled like a banshee. John Crossley's report in August mentioned more bad weather. When conditions improved, many workers went off to help in the hayfields of family and friends. Crossley fell ill but this dogged man returned to work a few weeks later. Even more work fell on the two *Midland* stalwarts of Contract No 1—Edgar O Ferguson (resident engineer) and W H Ashwell (agent and manager). "Under the general direction of these gentlemen, about three thousand labourers have long been engaged with steady perseverance in overcoming natural difficulties which at times seemed hopeless and insurmountable."

For every large structure, there were a dozen smaller ones which received little publicity, including an arched bridge built over Little Dale Beck, in the area where a tramway had operated from quarries in Littledale. The bed of the beck was lowered to accommodate the bridge. *Wildman's Household Almanack* for 1875 reported: "Solid stone has to be blasted to allow this to be done, but it will shortly be finished as a strong gang of men are at work on it."

On the positive side, the autumn of 1874 saw the construction of cottages at Salt Lake. A writer in *Household Almanack* wrote: "The erection of such structures shows a wise policy, as unless the men are comfortably housed it will be a difficult task to keep them at their various posts in the solitary and dreary places through which the line passes." The brightest event that autumn was a grand concert held in the Schoolroom at Batty Green for the benefit of Leeds Infirmary. On New Year's Day, 1875, a blizzard, one of the fiercest within living memory, swept the line. The road from Ingleton to Batty Green was overblown with deep drifts and traffic ceased. April brought a spell of fine weather and signalling was installed over much of the Settle-Carlisle. On the 29th, an inspection saloon carried the *Midland* directors over the line, most of which had been laid with at least a single permanent track.

On May 25th, the long-lasting dispute between the *Midland* and the Settle Highway Board with regard to the Chapel-le-Dale road was concluded, with the *Midland* agreeing to pay £100 towards its restoration. That same month, the auction sale of contractor's plant ("another unmistakable proof of the finish of work") began at Settle. A special train was run from Leeds, stopping on the way at Shipley, Keighley and Skipton. "Upon their arrival at Settle, the company (numbering about 200 passengers) found large quantities of working "plant" arranged in no fewer than 1,200 lots on both sides of the line for a distance of nearly a mile from the new station.

"The collection, as may be supposed, was a heterogeneous one, including a locomotive, boilers, engines, upwards of 70 wagons, 400,000 bricks, nearly 400 tons of contractor's rails, more than 100 tons of scrap iron and 800 tons of firewood, as well as other articles less known to the general public, and variously described as 'Goliaths', 'overhead travellers', &c. The whole of this accumulation belonged to what is distinguished as the first contract, and its sale is expected to realise something like £10,000. The auctioneeers are Messrs Oliver, Son and Appleton, of Leeds, who will continue the sale during the week... Among the first lot put up for the bid of purchasers was a large quantity of timber which had been used for huts in the now diminished navvy village at Batty Green.''

Without much fuss, on August 3, the first goods trains began their scheduled runs over the line, though only a single track existed between Hawes Junction and Mallerstang. Ten years had elapsed since Crossley had been authorised to plan the new route. The *Midland* directors recommended a dividend on ordinary stock for the half year at the rate of 6 per cent per annum. They no longer had to pay rent, estimated at between £70,000 and £80,000 per annum, for running powers over the *Lancaster-Carlisle* line. Blea Moor was provided with sidings to accommodate goods trains when the crack expresses were at their heels. Here, too, stood a signal box, water tank and two cottages to be used by signalmen and platelayers.

Many of the huts at Ribblehead had been removed and a good proportion of the labour force, and their families, drifted away to other jobs. The *Midland* withdrew its four policemen and now the duty of patrolling the line from Horton-in-Ribblesdale to Dent Head and back, a distance of twenty miles, fell on PC Walker. He did the walk ''through a very wild and hilly country'' every other day. The Scripture Readers on Contract No 1 left during the summer, having been given three months' notice and a gratuity of £10. The Mission at Batty Green was converted into two huts. At Ingleton Petty Sessions, on September 24th, Samuel Mathers of the *Welcome Home,* Batty Green, had his licence withdrawn. The need for the wooden inn had ended with the completion of the railway.

The hutment at Batty Green was intact, but many huts had been dismantled at different sites between here and Blea Moor. The remaining men and their families were simply transferred to Batty Green. Men who had work to do on the line were transported to and fro by locomotive. The steel rails, made by the Bessemer process, rested on ballast made from rock removed from a limestone face near Salt Lake Cottages. Between Batty Green and Selside, a large labour force was directed to making a new road. On the south side of Selside, model cottages, similar to those at Salt Lake, were built for those who would work for the new railway.

In the autumn of 1875, a correspondent of the *Lancaster Guardian,* visiting the line, saw men pulling down the empty huts at Denthead. "In Blea Moor Tunnel (about a mile and a-half long) there were a few men working. When about half-way through, a fog signal made the engine driver greatly diminish his speed. Shortly we came to a number of workmen whose dimly-burning candles only made the deep excavation look more gloomy. The sounds of the shrill whistle of the engine were loud and discordant...On the south side of the Tunnel, a few cottages were being built for signalmen and other employees. There are many deep cuttings through clay and bog earth between the tunnel and Batty Moss Viaduct...On the south side of the Batty Green, the Ingleton-road station is in progress."

Local limestone was used for viaducts and bridges. The stations and stationmaster's houses were invariably built with "brown stone, of a very warm and pleasant tint." The stations "afford abundant accommodation for passengers." Slate and blue limestone featured in two rows of cottages built near Selside "for the use of the company's servants". A piece of land had been purchased so that the eight cottagers might have gardens. Half a mile south of Selside, a large pothole had been filled in and added largely to the size of the field in which it was situated. "The filling in this hole prevented all possibility of the embankment slipping. A tip wagon lies buried at the bottom as it accidentally slipped over. It would have been more expensive pulling it up than what it was worth.''

Snow crusted the high Pennines on May 1st, when the first passenger train of the regular service left Skipton at 7-15am and stopped at all the stations to Carlisle. At Settle, the Union Jack flew on Castleberg, the train exploded fog signals placed on the line and was greeted to the platforms by a large crowd. Settle-Carlisle still took its toll of human life. That same month, as recorded in the *Westmorland Gazette,* George Bryer, a stone-crusher with accommodation at Batty Wife Green, was walking in the four-foot of the line between Salt Lake and Selside when he was struck by a goods train. ''Being still alive when picked up, he was put into the goods train coming to Settle, but he died on the way.''

Farmers, shepherds and gamekeepers were the silent witnesses at Ribblehead and Blea Moor as *Midland* expresses, with their luxurious Pullman cars, ran smoothly across the big viaduct and on to where Blea Moor was pierced by a tunnel lying up to 500 feet below the heather-tousled moor. Wind, rain, frost and thaw, soon removed the obvious traces of the hutments. Grass began to grow over the site of the brickworks. What remained of the tramway was kept close-cropped and green by the moor sheep. The Pennine wind strummed the spoil heaps which, from a distance, looked like carbuncles on the face of Blea Moor.

At Chapel-le-Dale, the unmarked graves from ''railway time'' were grassed over and lichens appeared on the tombstones of the favoured few. It was said that the funeral of Henry Bachelor, in February, 1875, was the two hundred and tenth at this little church—not quite as many as took place in the chapelry during the hundred years prior to the making of the Settle-Carlisle. An obituary for August 5th, 1878, caused a ripple of interest in the district. John Crossley, architect of the Settle-Carlisle, had died at Barrow on Soar, Leicestershire, a part of England far removed in spirit from the wild Pennine uplands, the obstinate rock and soup-like boulder clay which had been his major concern during the last few years of his working life.